Acknowledgements

The author and Publishers would like to thank the Wellcome Institute in London for their help.

The Publishers would like to thank the following for permission to use illustrations:

Allsport, p.58 (bottom right); Action on Smoking and Health, pp.59 (all), 60 (bottom left, centre top and right); Bridgeman Art Library, pp.12, 61 (bottom); Richard Bristow, Barcelona (© OUP) p.45 (bottom); Camera Press, p.63 (right); Claydon House, Bucks p.31 (right); David Cochran, Glasgow (© OUP) pp.13 (right), 18 (bottom), 28 (top); Sally and Richard Greenhill, p.56; Hulton/Deutsch pp.36 (top and bottom left), 40 (bottom right), 50 (left), 53, 55 (both), 58 (top right); Imperial War Museum p.41 (right); Rob Judges, Oxford (© OUP) p.4; King's College Hospital, p.41 (top left); Kobal Collection, p.58 (bottom left); Mary Evans Picture Library, pp.14 (top), 19 (left), 21, 23, 29 (left), 35, 36 (bottom right), 37 (right), 57 (both), 58 (top left and top centre), 63 (left); Museum of the History of Science, Oxford, p.44 (left); Popperfoto, pp.8, 44 (right), 45 (top); Punch Picture Library, pp.34, 54; Save the Children Fund, p.17; Science Museum, London, pp.38 (top), 61 (top) (photo: Jarrolds Norwich); Science Photo Library p.42; Scottish Health Education Group p.60 (top left and bottom centre); Smith Kline Beecham Pharmaceuticals, p.46; University of Kent, Canterbury (Centre for the Study of Cartoons and Caricature), pp.47, 48, 49, 50 (centre and right), 51; Wellcome Institute, London, pp.4, 5, 6, 7, 11, 14 (bottom), 15 (both), 18 (top), 19 (right), pp.20, 22, 25, 27, 28 (bottom), 29 (right), 30, 31 (left), 32, 33, 38 (bottom), 39 (top), 40, 41 (bottom left), Webster and Oliver (photographers), Worcester, (© OUP), p.10 (bottom); Worcester Royal Infirmary, p.10 (top).

Cover illustration (from front to back): Wellcome Institute, Popperfoto

Oxford University Press, Walton St, Oxford OX2 6DP

Oxford New York Toronto
Delhi Bombay Calcutta Madras Karachi
Petaling Jaya Singapore Hong Kong Tokyo
Nairobi Dar es Salaam Cape Town
Melbourne Auckland

and associated companies in
Berlin Ibadan

Oxford is a trademark of Oxford University Press

© Oxford University Press 1990

ISBN 0 19 913359 X

Typesetting by MS Filmsetting Limited,
Frome, Somerset
Printed in Hong Kong

Studies in British Social and Economic History

Series Editor: Peter Mathias

Medical Care and Public Health

1780 to the present

Alastair McIntosh Gray

Oxford University Press 1990

Studies in British Social and Economic History

Introduction

This series is designed to confront the principal objectives of GCSE history and to provide practical schemes of work which include sources of historical evidence, questions, and mark schemes.

Several assumptions underpin the series. Firstly, evidence is seen to be at the heart of historical study. The evidence in this book comes from a wide range of sources. Each chapter is a unique combination of sources selected to encapsulate, as far as possible, an aspect of the work of the historian. Whereas this book cannot claim to enable students to pursue an exhaustive study of available evidence, the evidence has been selected to provide breadth and balance within the scope of each exercise.

Secondly, the evidence has been selected with a particular historical skill in mind. It will be seen that each chapter is double-headed. The whole book covers fourteen major topics in the history of medical care and public health in Britain, but at the same time uses the individual material of each of these chapters to pursue a particular historical objective. At the end of each chapter can be found questions which meet the coursework requirements of GCSE examining boards.

Content has often been discussed in the recent historical debate. This series shows how skills and content can complement each other to produce effective and highly motivated learning in history.

Contents

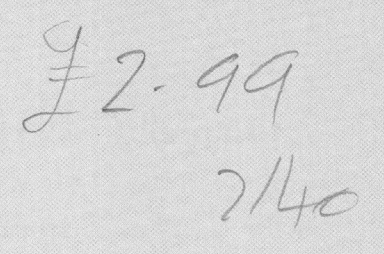

Chapter 1	The decline of smallpox *An exercise in the interpretation of evidence*	4
Chapter 2	The growth of the voluntary hospitals *An exercise in historical judgement*	9
Chapter 3	A need for bodies *An exercise in the analysis and synthesis of evidence*	12
Chapter 4	Cholera and public health reform *An exercise in the analysis and evaluation of evidence*	17
Chapter 5	General practitioners in the nineteenth century *An exercise in the interpretation and evaluation of fiction and art as historical sources*	22
Chapter 6	Mental illness *An exercise in causation*	26
Chapter 7	Florence Nightingale *An exercise in the analysis and evaluation of secondary sources*	30
Chapter 8	The reform of workhouse nursing *An exercise in the interpretation of evidence*	34
Chapter 9	Safer surgery *A study of change and continuity*	38
Chapter 10	Penicillin – Fleming and Florey *An exercise in historical judgement*	42
Chapter 11	The creation of the National Health Service *An exercise in the use of cartoons as historical evidence*	47
Chapter 12	Women and childbirth *A study in the use of oral history as historical evidence*	52
Chapter 13	Cigarette smoking *An exercise in the interpretation and evaluation of advertisements as historical evidence*	57
Chapter 14	The role of medicine *An exercise in the interpretation of evidence*	61

Chapter 1 The decline of smallpox

An exercise in the interpretation of evidence

Smallpox is an extremely infectious disease, which can leave those who live through an attack hideously disfigured by the pox-marks ('pock-marks') it causes. In the eighteenth century perhaps half the population of Europe was pock-marked – evidence of having survived smallpox. One-fifth of all deaths in London in 1796 may have been caused by smallpox.

It had long been known that people who survived infectious diseases such as smallpox were partly protected or *immune* from further attack. The procedure of *inoculation* – deliberately giving a small dose of a disease to build up some immunity – was based on this knowledge. Inoculation against smallpox was introduced to England in 1721 and became quite widespread.

In the 1770s a Gloucestershire doctor called Edward Jenner noticed that the mild disease called cowpox also gave some immunity to the much more serious smallpox. In 1796 he introduced the technique of *vaccination*. Vaccination (*vacca* is Latin for cow) was similar to inoculation, but it was safer and cheaper, and unlike inoculation did not carry the risk of spreading smallpox to unprotected people.

This chapter looks at these new methods for fighting smallpox, and the gradual decline of the disease.

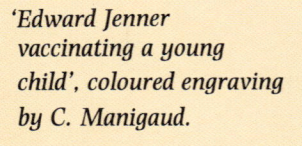

'Edward Jenner vaccinating a young child', coloured engraving by C. Manigaud.

A Lady Mary Wortley Montagu, wife of Britain's Ambassador to Turkey, lost her younger brother in 1713 from an attack of smallpox, and had herself been disfigured by an attack of it in 1715. In April 1717 she wrote a letter to an English friend describing something she had seen:

> The smallpox, so fatal and so general amongst us, is here entirely harmless by the invention of *ingrafting* ... the old woman comes with a nut-shell full of the matter of the best sort of smallpox, and asks what veins you please to have opened. She immediately rips open that you offer to her with a large needle ... and puts into the vein as much venom as can lie upon the head of her needle.... The children or young patients play together all the rest of the day, and are in perfect health to the eighth. Then the fever begins to seize them, and they keep their beds two days, very seldom three. They have very rarely above twenty or thirty (spots) in their faces, which never mark; and in eight days time they are as well as before their illness. Every year thousands undergo this operation ... There is no example of anyone who has died in it, and you may believe I am very well satisfied of the safety of the experiment, since I intend to try it on my dear little son. I am patriot enough to take pains to bring this useful invention into fashion in England....

B From *The Gentleman's Magazine*, March 1779:

> The royal family, nobility, and people of fortune, have now their children inoculated at proper ages; the people too in middle life inoculate pretty generally; and the poor ... are everywhere desirous of being inoculated as soon as the natural smallpox begins to rage near them.

C Dr Edward Jenner describing in 1801 his discovery:

> My inquiry into the nature of Cow Pox commenced upwards of twenty-five years ago. My attention to this singular disease was first excited by observing, that among those whom in the country I was frequently called upon to inoculate, many resisted every effort to give them the smallpox. These patients I found had undergone a disease they called the Cow Pox, contracted by milking cows affected with a peculiar eruption on their teats. On inquiry, it appeared that it had been known among the dairies time immemorial, and that a vague opinion prevailed that it was a preventive of the Small Pox.
> I selected a healthy boy, James Phipps, and matter from the sore of Sarah Nelmes' hand was inserted on May 14th 1796 into the arm of the boy by means of two small cuts. The same boy was inoculated the first of July with matter taken from a smallpox pustule, but no disease followed.

D *A coloured engraving, by William Skelton after William Cuff, comparing the daily development of cowpox and smallpox pustules.*

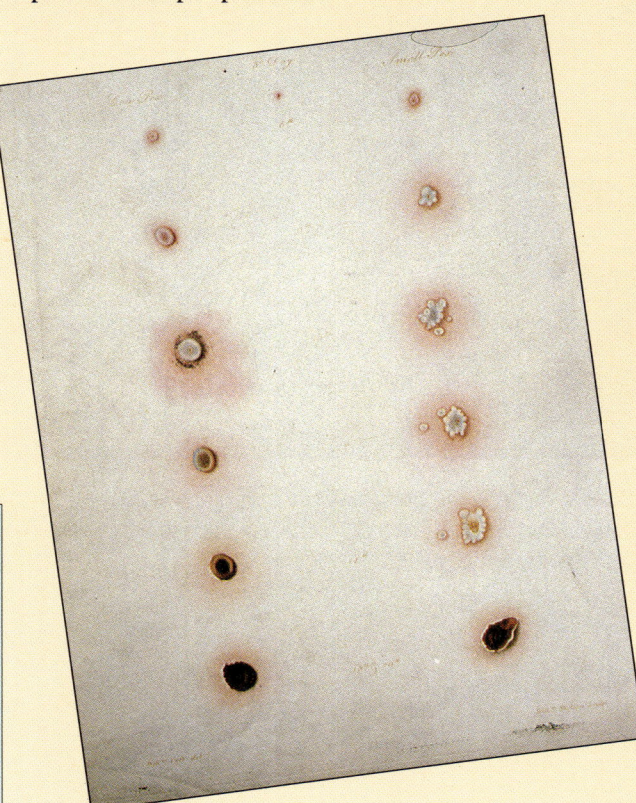

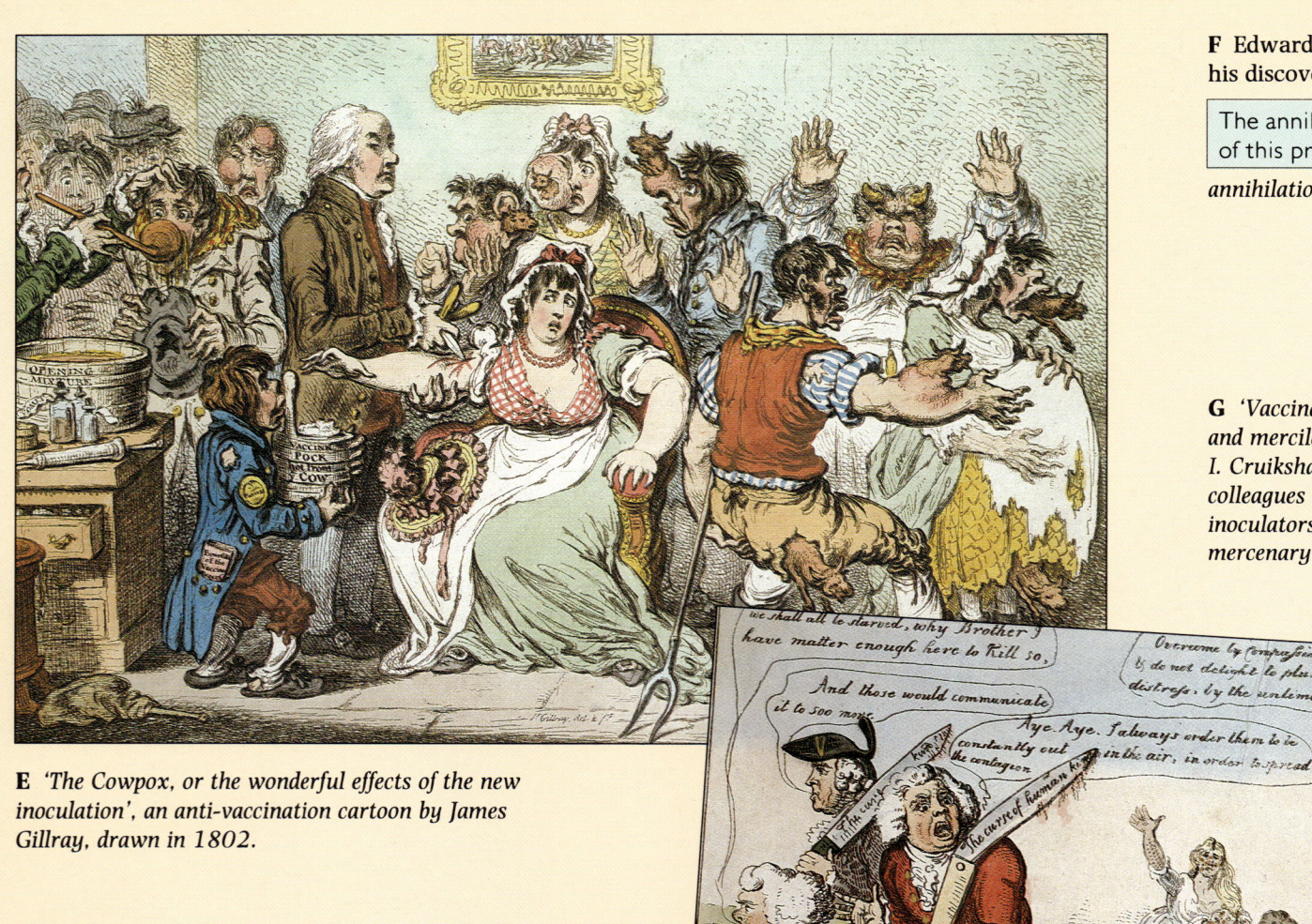

E *'The Cowpox, or the wonderful effects of the new inoculation', an anti-vaccination cartoon by James Gillray, drawn in 1802.*

F Edward Jenner, predicting in 1798 the effect of his discovery:

> The annihilation of smallpox must be the final result of this practice.

annihilation = destruction

G *'Vaccination against smallpox, or mercenary and merciless spreaders of death', a cartoon by I. Cruikshank from 1808 showing Jenner and two colleagues (on the right) displacing three smallpox inoculators (on the left).*
mercenary = working only for money

H *Two photographs showing a man from Gloucester during (below) and after (right) an attack of smallpox in 1896. An epidemic of smallpox in Gloucester that year killed 192 unvaccinated people, but only one of whom was vaccinated.*

I From *Endangered Lives: Public Health in Victorian Britain*, by Anthony Wohl, 1983:

The Victorian state did not impose compulsory vaccination on the nation without first going through a trial period of voluntary vaccination. The smallpox epidemic of 1837–40, in which almost 42,000 people died, represented a challenge which had to be met: the response was a *permissive* vaccination act (1840) which enabled anyone to be vaccinated at public expense ... it was not until 1853 ... that a *compulsory* vaccination act was passed. This made it obligatory for parents to have their infants vaccinated within three months of birth.

... Not unexpectedly a powerful anti-vaccination movement sprang up ... on both religious and political grounds it was argued that the rights of the individual had to be defended against this new menace of a doctoring state ... it was maintained that the individual must be allowed to take his chance on death ...

J *Graph showing the smallpox death rate in England and Wales. Smallpox declined in England during the nineteenth century, but it remained a serious problem in many countries.*

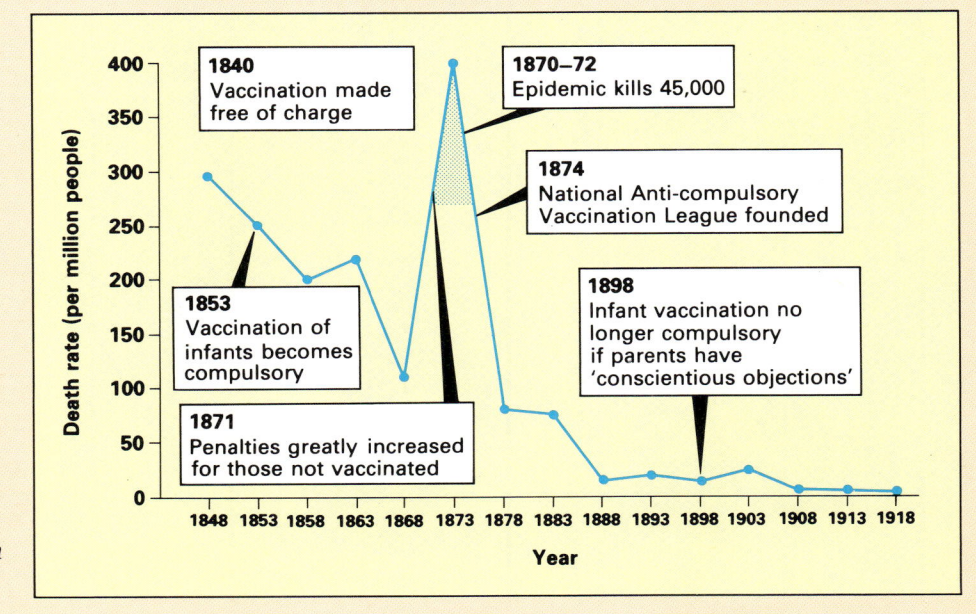

- **1840** Vaccination made free of charge
- **1853** Vaccination of infants becomes compulsory
- **1871** Penalties greatly increased for those not vaccinated
- **1870–72** Epidemic kills 45,000
- **1874** National Anti-compulsory Vaccination League founded
- **1898** Infant vaccination no longer compulsory if parents have 'conscientious objections'

K From *From the Face of the Earth*, by June Goodfield, 1985:

Larry Brilliant (an American doctor working in India during the 1970s on the World Health Organization's campaign to eradicate smallpox) ... found himself one night watching as an Indian government team broke into an adobe hut in the village where vaccination was being fiercely resisted, and a man and his entire family were forcibly vaccinated against the verbal and physical protests of Mohan Singh, the leader of the Ho tribe ... Mohan Singh said: 'Only God can decide who gets sickness and who does not. It is my duty to resist your interference within his will. We must resist your needles ...'.

Zafar Hussain (Brilliant's Muslim assistant) then spoke: 'these vaccinators are of your tribe. They also share your faith. But what is God's will? Is it God's will that you go hungry or that you plant rice and eat? Is it God's will that you go naked or that you make cloth and cover yourself? Look around you at your children. How many are absent today, dead from smallpox? That one over there is blind forever. Smallpox can be stopped with this vaccine. Must we all produce four children so that two will survive smallpox? I think it is God's will that our people don't suffer any more ... that we take vaccination'. Reaching hold of Brilliant's arm Zafar Hussain vaccinated him, for about the hundredth time, and then beckoned an elderly man on the fringe of the crowd and pleaded gently: 'We are not the enemy. Please take the vaccination'. The man stepped forward, and in the dawn, five hundred villagers were vaccinated.

eradicate = get rid of   adobe = sun-dried clay brick

L *Photograph of a parade going through New Delhi, India, in the 1960s, urging people to get vaccinated. In 1966 the World Health Organisation launched a campaign to rid the whole world of smallpox. The last case was diagnosed in 1977 and the world was declared to be smallpox-free in 1980.*

Questions

1. **a** Read Source **A** carefully. What evidence is there of Lady Montagu's personal interest in encouraging the adoption of inoculation in England?   3
   b What aspects of inoculation as described in Source **A** may have put people off being inoculated?   4
   c According to Source **B**, how widespread had inoculation become in England in 1779?   2
2. Examine Sources **C** and **D**. How scientific was Jenner's discovery of the cowpox vaccination against smallpox?   6
3. What messages are Sources **E** and **G** trying to put across, and what techniques or devices have been used to convey these messages?   7
4. How far do Sources **H**, **I**, **J**, **K**, and **L** support Jenner's prediction in Source **F**?   4
5. What similarities can you find in Sources **I** and **K** about the arguments against vaccination?   4

Chapter 2 The growth of the voluntary hospitals

An exercise in historical judgement

Until the eighteenth century there were virtually no hospitals in England, except for small alms-houses and hospices that had been established by charity or were attached to religious institutions. From 1720 onwards, however, a wave of new hospital building spread across the country. By 1800 almost all cities and towns of any size had their own hospital. These hospitals were built with private money given voluntarily, and so came to be known as voluntary hospitals. The sources in this chapter trace their growth.

A Part of a Declaration by 78 citizens in Bristol in 1736:

> Whereas many sick persons languish and die miserably for want of necessaries ... and are sometimes lost partly for want of accommodation and proper medicines in their own houses and lodgings ... and by the ignorance or ill-management of those about them — we whose names are underwritten (in obedience to the rules of our holy religion) desiring ... to find some remedy for this great misery of our poor neighbours — do subscribe the following sums of money, to be by us continued yearly during pleasure, for ... an Infirmary at Bristol for the benefit of the poor sick, who shall be recommended by any of the Subscribers or Benefactors in such manner as the majority of them shall direct.

(The Infirmary opened in Bristol the following year).

languish = grow feeble
infirmary = hospital
subscribers and benefactors = people who have given money or other help

B *A donation board in the Radcliffe Infirmary, Oxford, showing the names of subscribers and the amounts given.*

C Part of the Regulations at York County Hospital, 1743:

> Ordered That a Subscriber of One Pound per Annum shall be allowed to have One Out-Patient on the Hospital book at a time, and no more; and that a Subscriber of Two Pounds per Annum shall be allowed one Out, or one In patient at a Time, and no more; and that a subscriber of Three pounds per Annum shall be allowed one Out and one In Patient at a time.

D From a Sermon by Richard Meadowcroft in 1753, on the anniversary of the founding of the Worcester Royal Infirmary:

> As for those generous Benefactors to the Poor and the Publick who first laid the Foundations of the Worcester Infirmary and have contributed to raise it to its present state of Strength and Usefulness, they neither seek nor stand in need of Praise. Their works praise them.

E *A modern photo of the Worcester Royal Infirmary (Castle Street branch), still in use in the 1990s as a general hospital.*

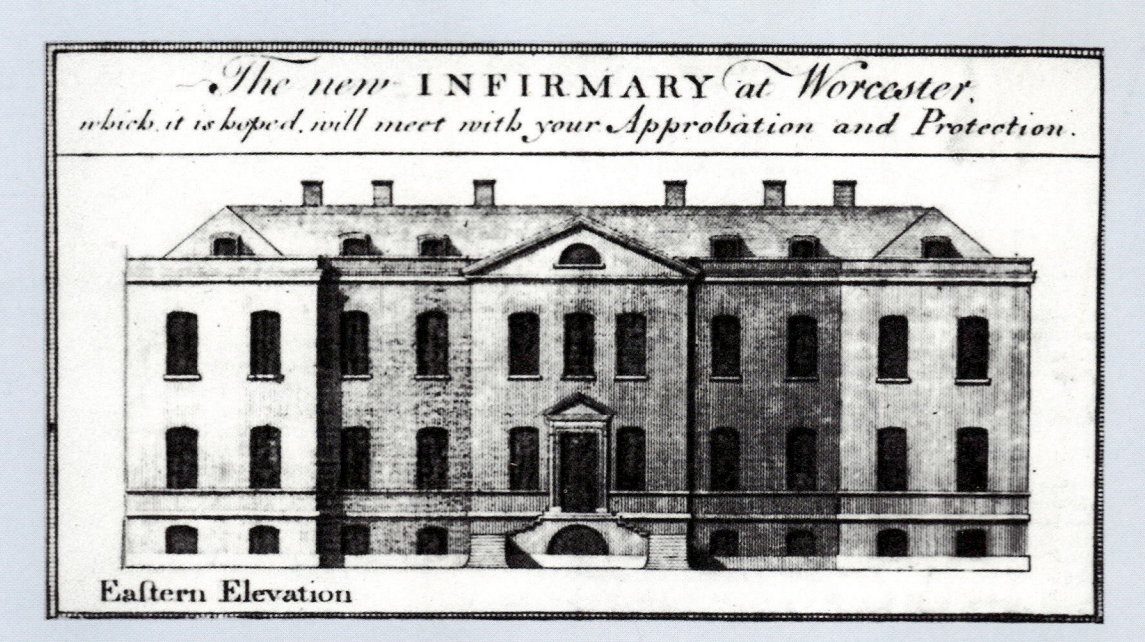

F *Part of the plans for a new infirmary at Worcester, drawn in 1767. The building was opened in 1771.*

G From a sermon preached in the Cathedral at Hereford in 1797, to the subscribers to the Hereford General Infirmary:

> To substitute hope for despair, to alleviate the poignancy of unexpected distress – to soothe affliction – and to administer comfort on the bed of despondency and sickness – are actions which every generous mind must feel a pleasure in performing. It is yours to distribute these blessings around you, and yours to enjoy the satisfactory result.

alleviate the poignancy = relieve the pain
despondency = loss of hope
affliction = misery, pain

H A suggested prayer for patients at Guy's Hospital, London:

Bless all the worthy Governors of this hospital; excite in our hearts a grateful sense of their charitable care for our welfare, and grant that they may plentifully reap the reward of their labour and love, both in this life and that which is to come.

I From *The Crisis of the Hospitals in the Industrial Revolution*, by Charles Webster, 1978:

The voluntary hospitals were an object of human pride, a conspicuous symbol of the charitable impulses of the rich, and a spur to the gratitude and submission of the poor.

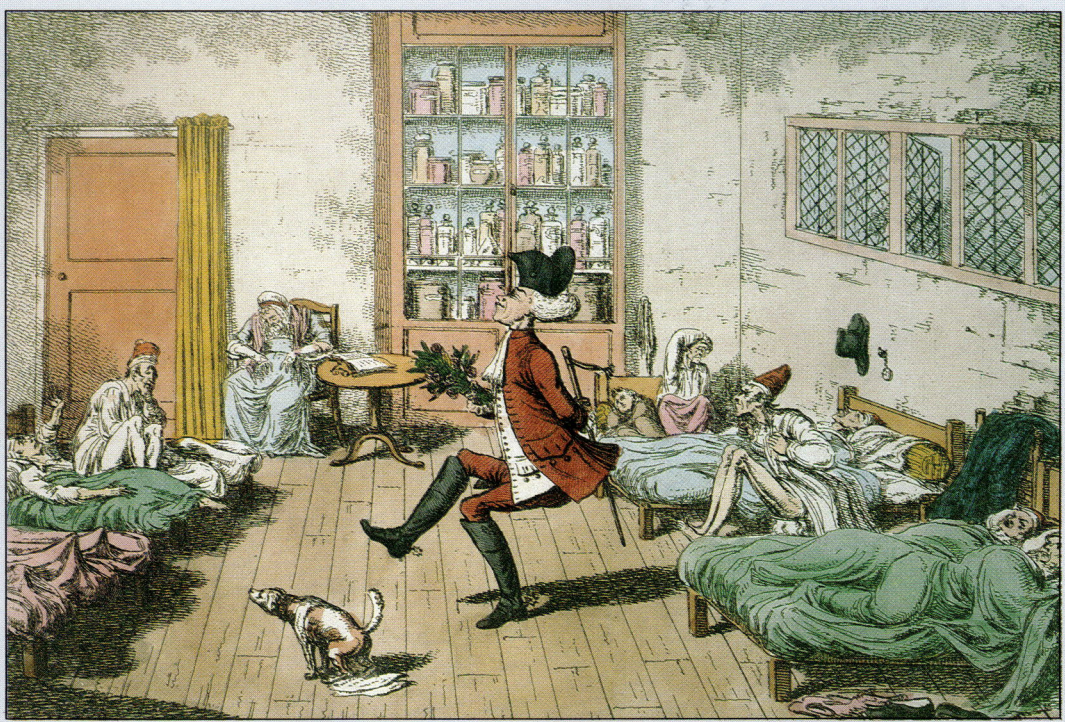

J *An etching from 1813 showing a ward in a country infirmary.*

M From a description of a visit in 1864 to the Royal Portsmouth, Portsea, and Gosport Hospital:

> It is difficult to avoid a feeling of very great regret on seeing an institution ... in a busy and crowded town like Portsmouth used mainly as a refuge for a few invalids who have had the good luck to recommend themselves to some subscriber.

N From *The Hospitals 1800–1948*, by Brian Abel-Smith, 1964:

... although infectious diseases were the great killers of the poor and the main menace for the rich, there was only one hospital for fever cases and one for smallpox cases in the whole of London ... As more epidemics raged across Britain's large and growing cities, more and more hospitals were excluding the victims. Thus, both for cases of infectious disease and for cases of chronic illness, the voluntary hospitals offered grossly inadequate accommodation. What was left undone by charity had eventually to be undertaken by public authorities.

L *One of the rules at Guy's Hospital, London, around 1800:*

> Patients are to be admitted on Thursday in every week at eleven o'clock of the forenoon precisely.

K The rules laying down who should be admitted to the Salop Infirmary, 1859:

> That no woman big with child, no child under seven years of age (except in extraordinary cases, such as fractures, stone, or where couching, trepanning or amputation is necessary), no persons disordered in their senses, suspected to have smallpox or other infectious distemper, having habitual ulcers, cancers not admitting to operation, epileptic or convulsive fits, consumptions, or dropsied in their last stage, in a dying condition, or judged incurable, be admitted as inpatients, or inadvertently admitted, be suffered to continue.

stone = a hard object that can form in the bladder
couching = a surgical procedure to remove a cataract from the eye
trepanning = an operation in which part of the skull is sawn open, for example to relieve severe head pains
amputation = the cutting off of part of the body, usually a limb
distemper = disorder or disease
consumption = tuberculosis
dropsied = suffering from a build-up of body fluid

Questions
1 a Read Source **A**. Explain the reasons it gives for establishing voluntary hospitals. 6
  b Read Source **I**, and look at Sources **A, B, C, D, E, F, G**, and **H**. How well does Source **I** summarise the motives for establishing voluntary hospitals given in Sources **A** to **H**? 16
2 Look at Sources **J, K, L, M**, and **N**. Describe the kinds of patients admitted to and excluded from the voluntary hospitals according to these sources. 8

11

Chapter 3 A need for bodies

An exercise in the analysis and synthesis of evidence

Modern medicine and surgery are based on detailed knowledge of the human body and the way it works. This knowledge cannot be obtained without dissecting bodies and examining them closely. From the sixteenth century onwards, the only bodies that English anatomists were legally allowed to dissect were those of hanged murderers. This was as much a final punishment of the murderers as a way to advance medical knowledge. By the eighteenth century medical schools were growing, and anatomists found it hard to obtain the bodies they needed. This led to the appearance of body-snatchers and grave-robbers, who stole buried corpses and sold them to the anatomists. Opposition grew, and finally in 1832 Parliament was forced to introduce a new law, by which the body of any pauper who died in a workhouse or hospital and was too poor to pay for a funeral was handed over to the anatomists.

A *'The Anatomy Lesson of Doctor Tulp', painted by Rembrandt in 1632. The painting was commissioned by the Amsterdam College of Surgeons.*

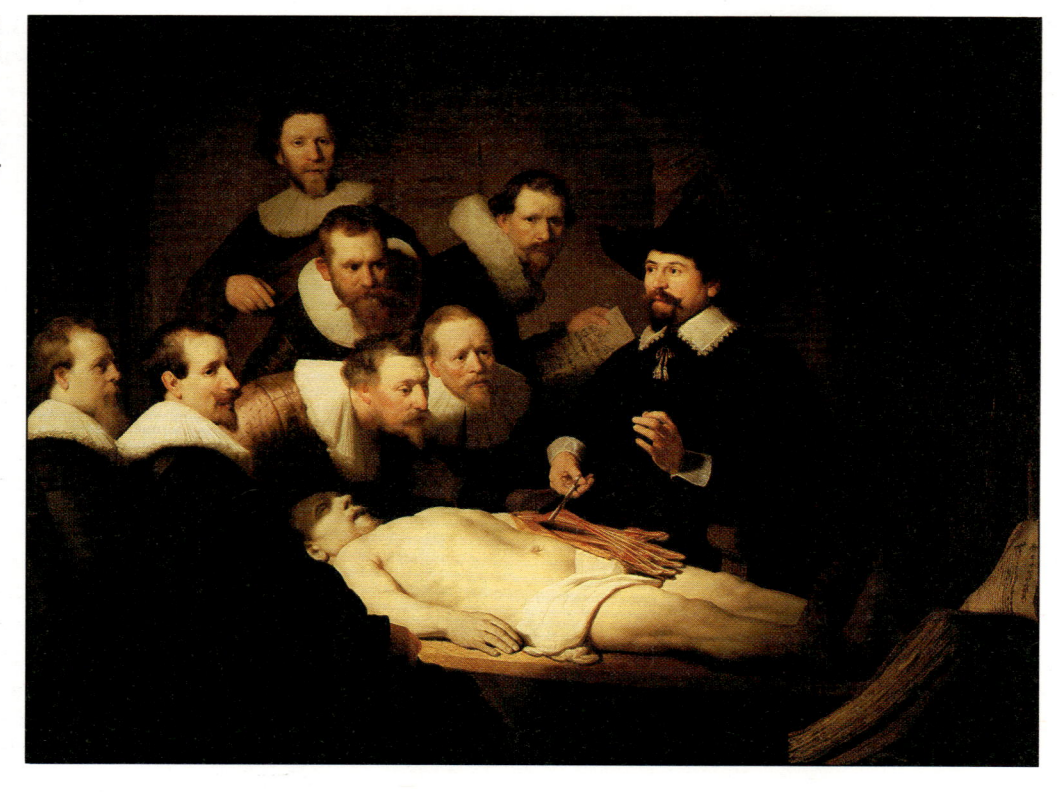

B *'The Fourth Stage of Cruelty', 1751, by William Hogarth, showing an official dissection at the Company of Surgeons.*

D *A modern photograph of an eighteenth century iron cage or 'mortsafe' over a grave in Greyfriars churchyard, Edinburgh, used to protect graves from body-snatchers. Edinburgh, with a large medical school and many medical students, needed a large supply of bodies for teaching anatomy, and so body-snatching was a big problem in the city.*

F In February 1795 three men were discovered leaving the St Thomas's burial ground in London carrying five bodies in sacks:

> ... in consequence of such a discovery, people of all descriptions, whose relatives had been buried in that ground, resorted thereto, and demanded to dig for them ... being refused, they in great number forced their way in, and in spight of every effort the parish Officers could use, began like mad people to tear up the ground. (Many empty coffins were found.) Great distress and agitation of mind was manifest in every one, and some, in a kind of phrensy, ran away with the coffins of their deceased relations.

C From an introductory lecture to medical students by the famous surgeon Wiliam Hunter, around 1780:

> Anatomy is the Basis of Surgery; it informs the Head, guides the hand, and familiarizes the heart to a kind of necessary Inhumanity.

E From the Vestry Minutes of St Pancras Parish Church, London, 10 April 1787:

> It was resolved to appoint a proper watch for the churchyard, consisting of one man straight through the year, and an additional one in the winter. The watchman should have a blunderbuss, a bayonet fixt, with a supply of powder and balls, a greatcoat, lanthern and rattle.

G When the body-snatcher William Millard was caught and imprisoned, his wife Ann decided to write a book (published in 1825) exposing her husband's unpleasant trade and the many other respectable people who although involved in it had refused to defend him:

Who, even among the practitioners of medicine, does not shudder at the mere contemplation that the remains of all which was dear to him, of a beloved parent, wife, sister, or daughter, may be exposed to the rude gaze and perhaps to the *indecent jests* of unfeeling men, and afterwards be mutilated and dismembered in the presence of hundreds of spectators.

H *A medical student recognises his own mother. The engraving was made from around 1835.*

I From *Death, Dissection and the Destitute*, by Ruth Richardson, 1988:

Corpses were bought and sold, they were touted, priced, haggled over, discussed in terms of supply and demand, delivered, imported, exported, transported. Human bodies were compressed into boxes, packed in sawdust, packed in hay, trussed up in sacks, roped up like hams, sewn in canvas, packed in cases, casks, barrels, crates and hampers; salted, pickled, or injected with preservative. They were carried in carts and wagons, in barrows and steamboats; manhandled, damaged in transit, and hidden under loads of vegetables. They were stored in cellars and on quays. Human bodies were dismembered and sold in pieces, or measured and sold by the inch.

J From the *Select Committee on Anatomy*, taking evidence from the famous surgeon Sir Astley Cooper in 1828:

Question: Is it not distressing to men of character and education, as the teachers in the schools of anatomy are, to be obliged to have recourse to a violation of the law, in order to obtain a supply of bodies and perform their duty towards their students?

Answer: ... the great difficulty teachers have to contend with, is the management of those persons, and it is distressing to our feelings that we are obliged to employ very faulty agents to obtain a desirable end.

K Evidence from Sir Henry Halford, President of the Royal College of Physicians, to the *Select Committee on Anatomy*, 1828:

(The resurrectionists) ought not to be tolerated at all if possible, and for the reason I will now present to your minds: when there is a difficulty in obtaining bodies, and their value is so great, you absolutely throw a temptation in the way of these men to commit murder for the purpose of selling the bodies of their victims.

'Lateral View of a Partially Skinned Cadaver', a chalk drawing of a corpse by the artist Charles Landseer, 1815.

L A broadsheet printed in Edinburgh in 1829:

EXECUTION

A full and particular account of the execution of W BURKE, who was hanged at Edinburgh on Wednesday the 28th January, 1829; also, an account of his conduct and behaviour since his condemnation, and on the Scaffold.

Early on Wednesday morning the Town of Edinburgh was filled with an immense crowd of spectators, from all places of the surrounding country, to witness the execution of a Monster, whose crime stands unparalleled in the annals of Scotland: viz.-for cruelly murdering Margery McConegal, and afterwards selling her body to the Doctors in October last.

While this unhappy man was under sentence, he made the following confession: that he had been engaged in this murderous traffic from Christmas 1827, until the murder of the woman McConegal, in October last; during which period, he had butchered Sixteen of his fellow-creatures, and that he had no accomplice but Hare; – that they perpetrated these fearful atrocities by suffocation. When they succeeded in making their victims drunk, the one held the mouth and nostrils, whilst the other went upon the body, and in this manner was the woman Docherty killed: they then sold her body to Doctor – in his rooms and received payment at his house – and that they were never resurrectionists: all the bodies they sold being murdered except one, who died a natural death in Hare's house.

M *Portraits of William Burke and his associate Helen McDougal in 1829.*

N *'Burking Poor Old Mrs Constitution', a political cartoon by William Heath from 1829 which attacks prime minister Wellington by portraying him as Burke.*

O The execution of Burke, on 28 January 1829, was witnessed by Sir Walter Scott:

> The mob, which was immense, demanded Knox and Hare, but, though greedy for more victims, received with shouts the solitary wretch who found his way to the gallows out of the five or six who seem not less guilty than he.

P From the *Report of the Select Committee on Anatomy*, 1829:

> It is the opinion of almost all the witnesses ... that the bodies of those who during life have been maintained at the public charge, and who die in workhouses, hospitals, and other charitable institutions, should, if not claimed by next of kin within a certain time after death, be given up, under proper regulations, to the anatomist; and some of the witnesses would extend the same rule to the unclaimed bodies of those who die in prison, penitentiaries, and other places of confinement ...

Q Robert Gooch, a gynaecologist, writing in the *Quarterly Review* in 1830:

> ... there are only three plans from which to select: one, to prohibit the study of anatomy altogether, and cause surgery to relapse into the infancy of the art: another, to support the breed of resurrection-men, plunder graves, and after all, supply the nation with half-informed anatomists and unskilful surgeons; the last is to give up unclaimed bodies to the schools of anatomy, by which resurrection-men would be abolished, the buried lie quietly in their graves, and the nation would be supplied with an ample stock of expert anatomists and dexterous surgeons.

R William Cobbett, the Radical campaigner, writing in 1832:

> .. the unfortunate persons who die in poor houses and hospitals have, in numerous cases seen better days, and have, during many years, contributed in direct payments towards the maintenance of the poor and the sick ... therefore, when he becomes so poor, helpless and destitute, as to die in a poor house or in a hospital, it is unjust, cruel, barbarous to the last degree, to dispose of his body to be cut up like that of a murderer!

T William Roberts, a London surgeon, led the campaign against the Anatomy Act of 1832, even after it had been passed:

> It is a point not to be lost sight of, that all classes of the community had their share of the annoyance (of body-snatching); all were liable to be reached by it. By the Bill of 1832, the upper and middle classes were protected, while the poor alone were left exposed.

U A modern anatomy room. Dissection is still an important part of a medical student's training. Here an autopsy is being watched by a student, who at various times has to answer questions on what he sees and the possible causes of death.

S *Graph showing sources of bodies used for dissection, 1935–1975.*

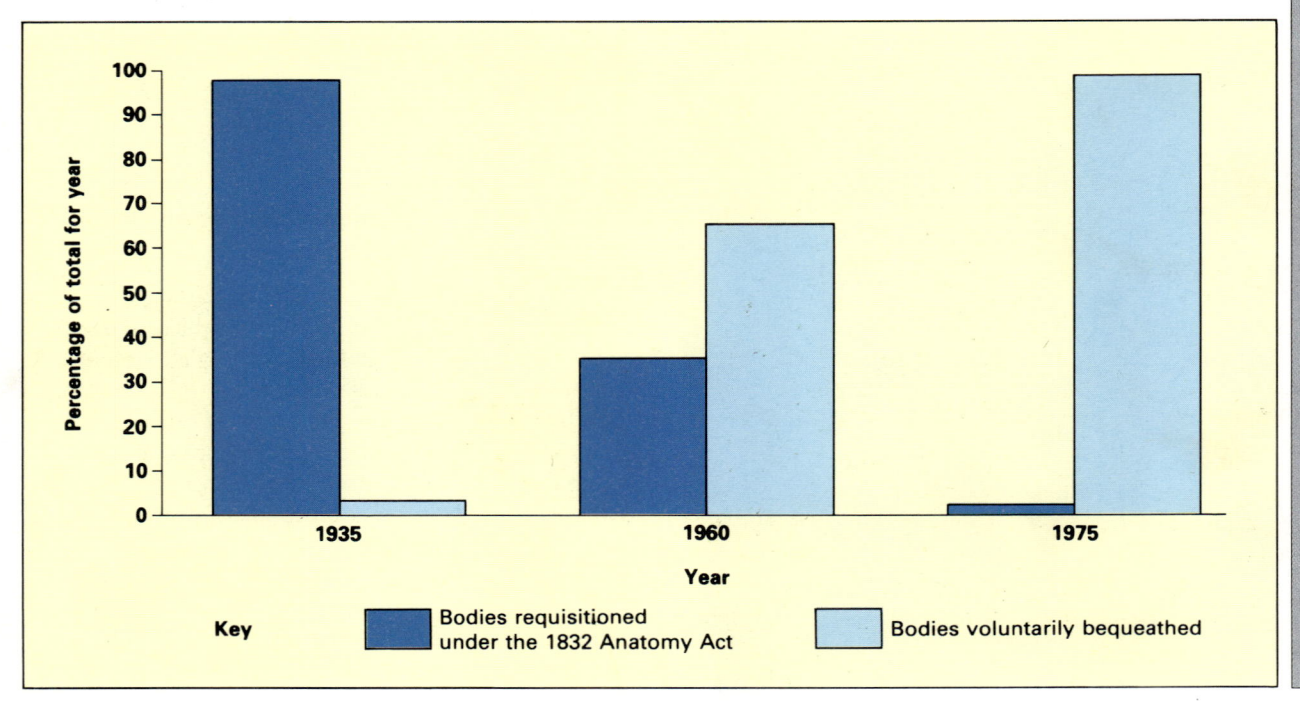

Key:
- Bodies requisitioned under the 1832 Anatomy Act
- Bodies voluntarily bequeathed

Questions

1. What might a comparison of Sources **A** and **B** reveal about changes in standards of anatomy teaching? — 3
2. What do you think William Hunter meant in Source **C**? (You may wish to refer back to Sources **A** and **B** in your answer). — 3
3. Refer to Sources **D–O**.
   a. What measures were taken to obtain bodies for anatomy. — 6
   b. What measures were taken to protect bodies from the body-snatchers? — 6
   c. What evidence can you find of the medical profession's attitude to body-snatching? — 5
4. Study Sources **P**, **Q**, **R**, and **T**. What solution was put forward to the body-snatching problem, and how acceptable was it? — 3
5. What do Sources **S** and **U** reveal about modern dissection? — 3

Chapter 4 Cholera and public health reform

During the nineteenth century cholera arrived in Britain for the first time. This infectious disease caused four serious epidemics which killed many people. Eventually it was realized that cholera was spread mainly by polluted water. Sewers and clean water supplies were installed, and the disease is now almost unknown in Britain. This chapter studies these events. Cholera is still a problem in many parts of the world, where a safe water supply remains the most urgent health need.

epidemic = a disease affecting a large number of people at the same time

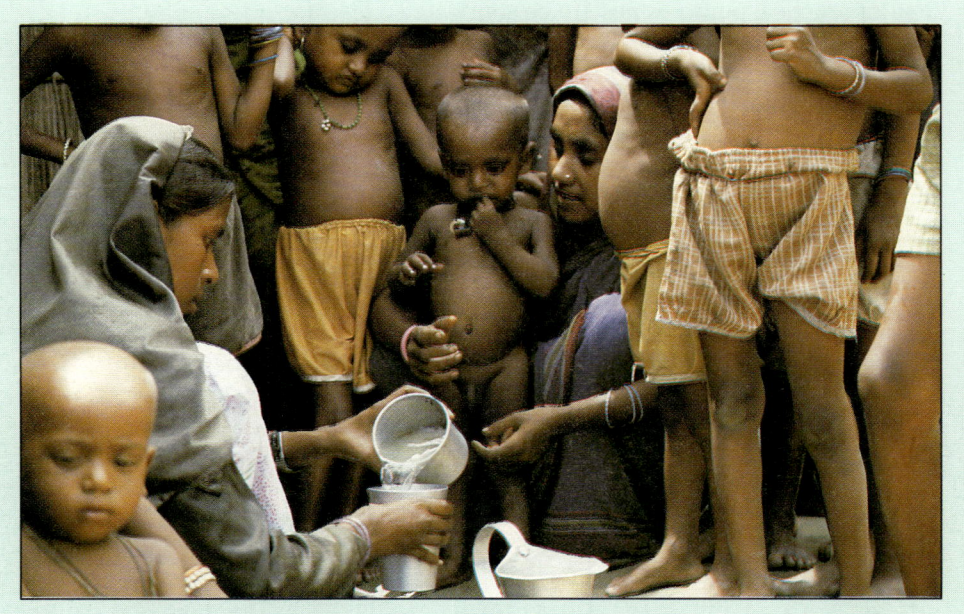

An oral rehydration solution being prepared for children in Bangladesh. Dehydration and water-borne diseases from poor water supplies are still a major cause of death in many countries of the world.

A From *Endangered Lives: Public Health in Victorian Britain*, by Anthony Wohl, 1983:

... cholera, a disease new to the English experience and the first national epidemic since the seventeenth century plague, served to remind the Victorians that their society, however progressive, was not immune to the scourges of the past.

... roughly 32,000 people died from cholera in (the first epidemic in) 1831–2, 62,000 in the epidemic of 1848–9, another 20,000 in 1853–4 and about 14,000 in 1866–7. But as important as the number dying was the high percentage of fatalities among those contracting the disease – between 40 and 60 per cent – and the speed with which cholera could strike. The victim could be dead within a few hours ...

scourges = miseries

B From the *Annual Register* of 1832:

The cholera left medical men as it had found them – confirmed in most opposite opinions, or in total ignorance as to its nature, its cure, and ... its origin ... or mode of transmission ...

C *A broadsheet, dated 1831, advising the inhabitants of Clerkenwell, London, of the symptoms and remedies of cholera.*

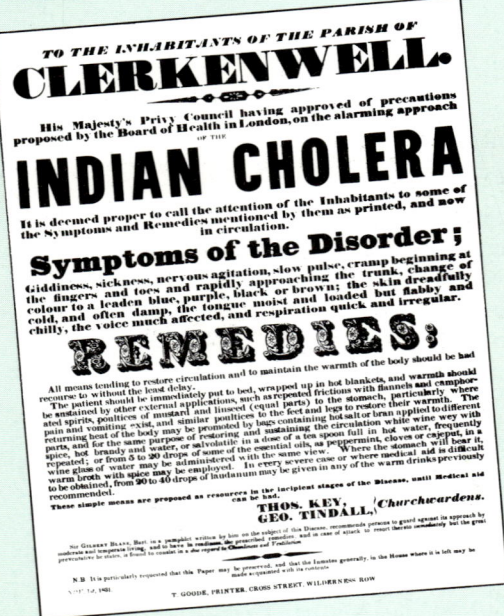

D *A cholera gravestone of 1832 in St Michael's Churchyard, Dumfries.*

E Edwin Chadwick, a Victorian civil servant, had no clearer idea than anyone else of the way cholera was transmitted. But he became convinced that dirt and disease went together, and set about proving this in his *Report on the Sanitary Conditions of the Labouring Population*. This account of his work is from *The Life and Times of Sir Edwin Chadwick*, by S. E. Finer, 1952:

Chadwick finished the Report by the end of 1841. ... its catalogue of horrors ... and his slow, laboured, patient evidence that health improved as such filthy conditions were abolished, impressed his public most forcibly. It alone made possible the adoption of the solution he outlined ...

'The medical controversy as to causes of fever', he wrote in the Report, 'does not appear to be one that for practical purposes need to be considered ... its effect is prejudicial in diverting attention from the practical means of prevention ... The great preventives, drainage, street and house cleansing by means of supplies of water and improved sewerage, and especially the introduction of cheaper and more efficient modes of removing all noxious refuse from the towns, are operations for which aid must be sought from the science of the *Civil Engineer*, not from the physician ...'.

controversy = argument
noxious = harmful

F From a description of the River Aire in 1840:

It was full of refuse from water closets, cesspools, privies, common drains, dunghill drainage, infirmary refuse, waste from slaughter houses, chemical soaps, gas, dyehouses and manufacturers; coloured by blue and black dyes, pig manure, old urine wash; there were dead animals, vegetable substances and occasionally a decomposed human body.

G From the *Report of Sanitary Conditions of the Labouring Population of Great Britain*, by Edwin Chadwick, 1842:

The mode of supplying water by private companies for the sake of profits is ... the subject of complaint in the populous towns, where it is the only mode. ... One (objection) is, that it creates strong interest against all improvements in the quality or the supplies of water; for every considerable improvement creates expense, which is felt in diminution of the dividends of the private shareholders ... It is a further subject of complaint, as respects supplies by such companies, that they are directed almost exclusively to the supplies of such private houses as can pay water-rates; that they are not arranged for the important objects of cleansing of the streets or drains ...

diminution of dividends = reduction in share of profits

H *An engraving of the new Fleet Street sewer being built in 1845, from the* Illustrated London News.

I *'The Water that John Drinks', a cartoon from* Punch, *1849.*

This is the water that JOHN drinks.

This is the Thames with its cento of stink,
That supplies the water that JOHN drinks.

These are the fish that float in the ink-
-y stream of the Thames with its cento of stink,
That supplies the water that JOHN drinks

This is the sewer, from cesspool and sink,
That feeds the fish that float in the ink-
-y stream of the Thames with its cento of stink,
That supplies the water that JOHN drinks.

These are vested int'rests, that fill to the brink,
The network of sewers from cesspool and sink,
That feed the fish that float in the ink-
-y stream of the Thames, with its cento of stink,
That supplies the water that JOHN drinks.

This is the price that we pay to wink
At the vested int'rests that fill to the brink,
The network of sewers from cesspool and sink,
That feed the fish that float in the ink-
-y stream of the Thames with its cento of stink,
That supplies the water that JOHN drinks.

cento = mixture

J From *A Social History of Medicine*, by F. F. Cartwright, 1977:

At the end of August 1849 cholera struck the district (around Golden Square in London) causing over 600 deaths. The outbreak took an explosive form in the Broad Street area ... John Snow (a London doctor) investigated eighty-nine deaths in Broad Street and found that all except ten of the dead lived close to the Broad Street pump and drew their water from the well. Of the remaining ten, five would have been expected to draw water from a nearer source but preferred the Broad Street supply. Three more were children who attended a school served by the pump ... Snow ... traced the pipelines of various water companies and showed that cholera abounded in districts served by one company but was almost absent in those served by another ... John Snow had proved that cholera is a water-borne disease ... he confirmed his findings during the epidemic of 1853–4.

K *'The New River Waterworks'*, a wood engraving showing the reconstruction of the storage reservoir at Claremont Square, London, from the *Illustrated London News, 22 November 1856.*

L *A modern version of part of John Snow's map showing deaths around the Broad Street pump. Each bar represents the number of deaths from cholera in a house.*

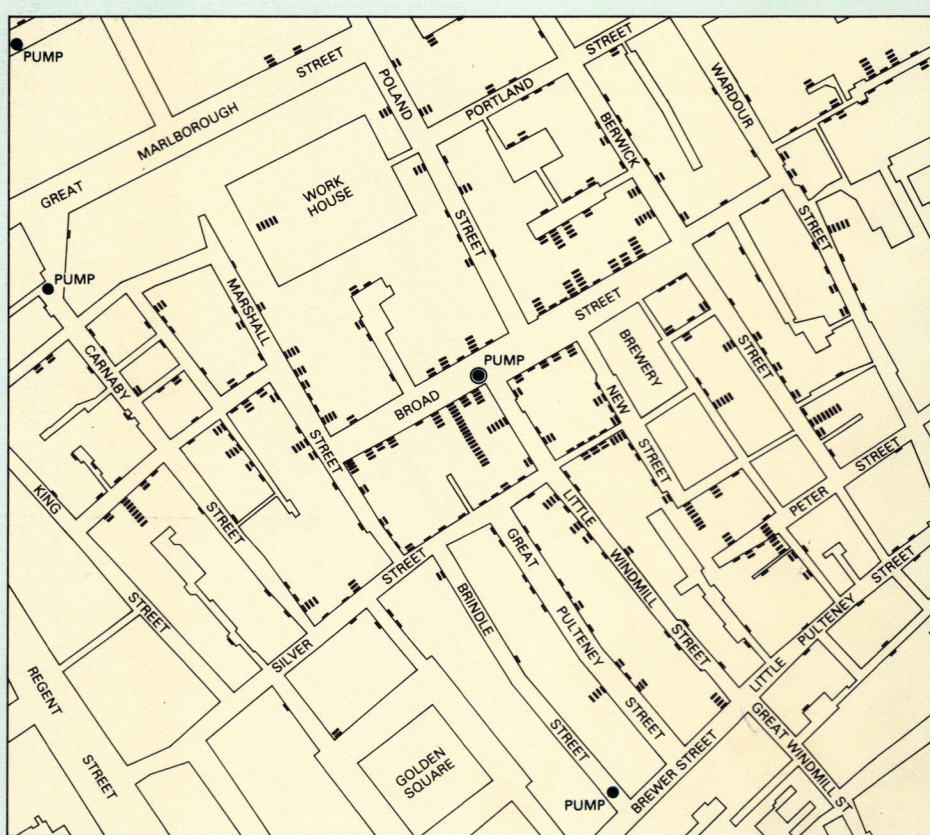

M *A cartoon by Tenniel in* Punch, *1858.*

FATHER THAMES INTRODUCING HIS OFFSPRING TO THE FAIR CITY OF LONDON.
(A Design for a Fresco in the New Houses of Parliament.)
DIPHTHERIA. SCROFULA. CHOLERA.

O *From the* Report on Cholera, 1866, *by William Farr:*

> In the interval between the year 1854 and the year 1866 the water of all the eight (London water) companies was taken from points higher up the rivers, and filtered, and following this, in 1866, cholera in every water-field was fatal to comparatively few when it visited London …

P *From* The People's Health 1830–1910, *by F. B. Smith, 1979:*

> … sanitary improvement could … have been implemented less tardily and patchily … Expenditure might well have been more prompt and lavish had the three great 'dirt' diseases among adults, Asiatic cholera, typhus, and typhoid, been less specific to the lower orders and been seen by middle class contemporaries to be so.

N *Table from the* Report on Cholera, 1866, *by William Farr, showing the number of deaths from cholera in parts of London during the epidemics of 1849, 1853–4, and 1866.*

District	Average house rent per person (£)	Number of deaths per 10,000 people 1849	1853–4	1866
Bermondsey	2.35	161	179	6
St George, Southwark	2.55	164	121	1
Newington	2.60	144	112	3
Rotherhithe	2.90	205	165	9
Average for all London	**5.00**	**62**	**46**	**18**
Kensington	6.30	24	38	4
St George, Hanover Square	11.40	18	33	2
St Martin-in-the-Fields	12.40	37	20	5
St James, Westminster	13.50	16	142	5

Questions

1. What evidence is contained in Sources **A**, **B**, **C**, and **D** to suggest why the arrival of cholera was so terrifying? 6
2. What do Sources **E**, **F**, **G**, **H**, and **I** reveal about the nature of the cholera problem and obstacles to reform? 10
3. Using Sources **J**, **K**, **L**, **M**, **N**, **O**, and **P**, evaluate the progress that was made in understanding cholera and making the reforms necessary to prevent it. 14

Chapter 5 General practitioners in the nineteenth century

An exercise in the interpretation and evaluation of fiction and art as historical sources

The sources in this chapter are all drawn from works of fiction or art which in various ways depict doctors during the nineteenth century.

A *'Time the Best Doctor', an etching by I. Cruikshank dated 1804.*

B Extracts from *The History of Pendennis*, by William Thackeray, 1848–50:

Early in the Regency of George the Magnificent, there lived in a small town in the west of England, called Clavering, a gentleman whose name was Pendennis. There were those alive who remembered having seen his name painted on a board, which was surrounded by a gilt pestle and mortar over the door of a very humble little shop in the city of Bath, where Mr Pendennis exercised the profession of apothecary and surgeon; and where he not only attended gentlemen in their sick-rooms, and the ladies at the most interesting periods of their lives, but would condescend to sell a brown-paper plaster to a farmer's wife across the counter – or to vend toothbrushes, hair powder, and London perfumery.

And yet that little apothecary ... was a gentleman of good education ... but in his second year at Oxbridge his father died insolvent, and poor Pen was obliged to betake himself ... into so odious a calling.

He quickly after his apprenticeship ... set up for himself at Bath with his modest medical ensign. He had for some time a hard struggle with poverty; and it was all he could do to keep the shop and its gilt ornaments in decent repair, and his bed-ridden mother in comfort: but Lady Ribstone, happening to be passing to the Rooms with an intoxicated Irish chairman who bumped her ladyship up against Pen's very door-post, and drove his chair-pole through the handsomest pink bottle in the surgeon's window, alighted screaming from her vehicle, and was accommodated with a chair in Mr. Pendennis's shop, where she was brought round with cinnamon and sal-volatile.

Mr Pendennis's manners were so uncommonly gentlemanlike and soothing, that her Ladyship ... appointed her preserver, as she called him, apothecary to her person and family, which was very large. ... from that day (he) began to prosper.

George the Magnificent = George IV (1820–1830)
odious = hateful
intoxicated = drunken
apothecary = chemist, dispenser of drugs
sal-volatile = smelling salts

C 'The Travelling Quack Doctor', portrayed in the magazine *The Leisure Hour*, 1866.

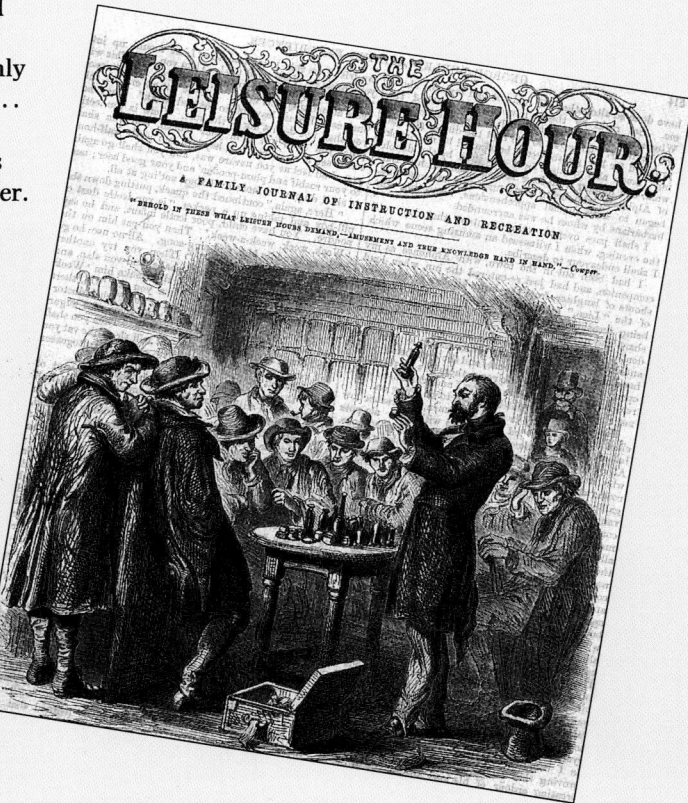

D *Middlemarch: A Study of Provincial Life*, by George Eliot, was first published in 1871–2, but is set during the years 1829–1832. In this extract Mr Lydgate, a doctor, is making a professional call to Mr Casaubon:

'Mr Lydgate', said Mr Casaubon, with his invariably polite air, 'I am exceedingly obliged to you for your punctuality. We will, if you please, carry on our conversation in walking to and fro'.

'I hope your wish to see me is not due to the return of unpleasant symptoms', said Lydgate, filling up a pause.

'Not immediately – no ... You have not implied to me that the symptoms which – I am bound to testify – you watched with scrupulous care, were those of a fatal disease. But were it so, Mr Lydgate, I should desire to know the truth without reservation, and I appeal to you for an exact statement of your conclusions: I request it as a friendly service.' ...

'Then I can no longer hesitate as to my course', said Lydgate ... 'I believe that you are suffering from what is called fatty degeneration of the heart, a disease which was first divined and explored by Laennec, the man who gave us the stethoscope, not so very many years ago. A good deal of experience – a more lengthened observation – is wanting on the subject. But after what you have said, it is my duty to tell you that death from this disease is often sudden. At the same time, no such result can be predicted ...'

'I thank you, Mr Lydgate', said Mr Casaubon ...

Lydgate, certain that this patient wished to be alone, soon left him; and the black figure with hands behind and head bent forward continued to pace the walk where the dark yew-trees gave him a mute companionship in melancholy ... Here was a man who now for the first time found himself looking into the eyes of death ...

E *'The Doctor', by Sir Luke Fildes, painted around 1890. The doctor seems not to know how to treat the sick child*

F Extracts from *Dr Thorne*, by Anthony Trollope, first published in 1858.

And thus Dr Thorne became settled for life in the little village of Greshamsbury. As was then the wont with many country practitioners, and as should be the wont with them all if they consulted their own dignity a little less and the comforts of their customers somewhat more, he added the business of a dispensing apothecary to that of physician. In doing so, he was of course much reviled.

There was much about this new comer which did not endear him to his own profession. In the first place he was a new comer, and, as such, was of course to be regarded by other doctors as being *de trop*. Greshamsbury was only fifteen miles from Barchester, where there was a regular depot of medical skill, and but eight from Silverbridge, where a properly-established physician had been in residence for the last forty years. Dr Thorne's predecessor at Greshamsbury had been a humble-minded general practitioner, gifted with a due respect for the physicians of the county; and he, though he had been allowed to physic the servants, and sometimes the children at Greshamsbury, had never had the presumption to put himself on a par with his betters.

Then, also, Dr Thorne ... made it known to the East Barsetshire world, very soon after he had seated himself at Greshamsbury, that his rate of pay was to be seven-and sixpence a visit within a circuit of five miles, with a proportionally-increased charge at proportionally-increased distances. Now there was something low, mean, unprofessional and democratic in this; so, at least, said the children of Aesculapius gathered together in conclave at Barchester. In the first place, it showed that this Thorne was always thinking about his money, like an apothecary, as he was, whereas it would have behoved him, as a physician, had he had the feelings of a physician under his hat, to have regarded his own pursuits in a purely philosophical spirit, and to have taken any gain which might have accrued as an accidental adjunct to his station in life.

And then it was clear that this man had no appreciation of the dignity of a learned profession. He might be seen compounding medicines in the shop, at the left hand of his front door; not making experiments philosophically ... but positively putting together common powders for rural bowels, or spreading vulgar ointments for agricultural ailments.

Now there was in this, it must be admitted, quite enough to make him unpopular among his brethren; and this feeling was soon shown in a marked and dignified manner. Dr Fillgrave, who had certainly the most respectable professional connection in the county, who had a reputation to maintain, and who was accustomed to meet, on almost equal terms, the great medical baronets from the metropolis at the houses of the nobility – Dr Fillgrave declined to meet Dr Thorne in consultation. He exceedingly regretted, he said, most exceedingly, the necessity which he felt of doing so: he had never before had to perform so painful a duty; but, as a duty which he owned to his profession, he must perform it.

Then, indeed, there was war in Barsetshire ... Dr Thorne addressed a letter to the *Barsetshire Conservative Standard*, in which he attacked Dr Fillgrave with some considerable acerbity. Dr Fillgrave responded in four lines ... and then the war raged merrily.

de trop = superfluous
physic = dose with medicine
Aesculapius = the Roman god of medicine
conclave = private meeting

G *'Sentence of Death', painting by John Collier from around 1900: the doctor is informing the patient that he has a fatal disease.*

Questions
1 What do each of the fictional Sources **B**, **D**, and **F** reveal about contemporary attitudes towards the status and capability of general practitioners. Give examples from the sources to explain your answers. 14
2 Examine Sources **A**, **C**, **E**, and **G**. How useful are they as evidence of the changing status of general practitioners during the nineteenth century? 10
3 Of what value might the fictional material in Sources **B**, **D**, and **F** be to the historian? Explain your answer with reference to the sources. 6

Chapter 6 Mental illness

An exercise in causation

During the nineteenth century there were dramatic changes in the care of the mentally ill. Instead of neglecting lunatics at home or locking them away in gaols or workhouses, the idea gradually emerged that the insane could be cured and should be treated. Many large new asylums were built, and the number of people classified as insane soared. The following sources illustrate these changes and the explanations that were proposed for the increase in insanity.

The Rake's Progress – The Madhouse, by William Hogarth, 1735. The scene is inside the old Bedlam mental asylum (The Old Bethlehem Hospital at Finsbury in London). The two ladies on the left have paid a small fee to enter the hospital and look at the lunatics, as was the custom.

A *Graph showing the number of people identified as insane in England and Wales from 1807 to 1890.*

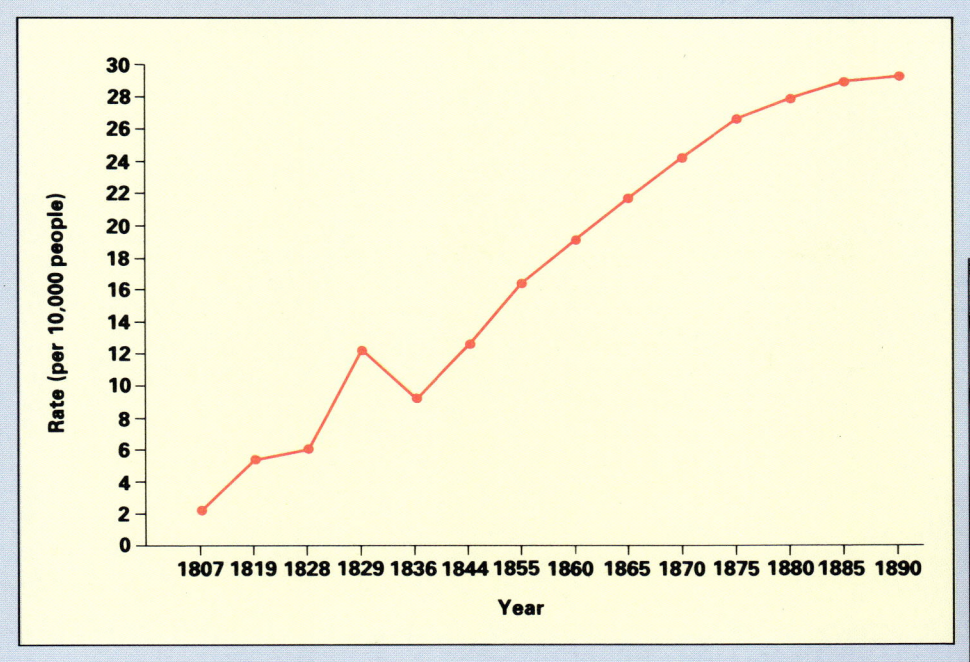

B From *Outlines of Mental Diseases*, by Alexander Morrison, 1824:

This leads to the question, whether insanity is on the increase or decrease? The former is said to be the case in this country, as both public and private establishments for the reception of the insane have increased. There can be little doubt that Insanity increases with civilization: in proof of which we find the number of insane stated to be very small in South America, and among the Indian tribes, etc., and to be very considerable in China. It is therefore probable, that the increasing civilization and luxury of this country ... tends rather to increase the numbers in proportion to the population.

C From *What Asylums Were, Are and Ought to Be*, by W. A. Browne, 1837:

... the occupations, amusements, follies and above all the vices of the present race are infinitely more favourable for the development of the disease (insanity) than any previous period.

D From the *Report of the Metropolitan Commissioners in Lunacy*, 1842:

Pauper lunatics have unfortunately become so numerous throughout the whole kingdom, that the proper construction and cost of asylums for their use has ceased to be a subject which affects a few counties only, and has become a matter of national interest and importance.

E *Engraving of an American called Norris who was found to have been chained for 12 years between 1802 and 1813 in his cell at Bedlam. 'Restraint' of patients had been the norm in the eighteenth century, but went out of favour in the nineteenth century.*

F *Modern photograph of the Sunnyside Royal mental hospital, Montrose, built in the mid-nineteenth century.*

H From the *Report of the Metropolitan Commissioners in Lunacy to the Lord Chancellor*, 1844:

> The disease ... of Lunacy is essentially different in its character from other maladies. In a certain proportion of cases, the patient neither recovers nor dies, but remains an incurable lunatic, requiring little medical skill in respect to his mental disease, and frequently living many years. A patient in this state requires a place of refuge ... so that a certain and progressive increase of chronic and incurable cases is produced ... A similar accumulation is taking place ... in nearly all the county Asylums.

G *'Twelfth-Night Entertainments at the Hanwell Lunatic Asylum', an anonymous wood engraving from the* Illustrated London News *of 1848. The psychiatrist John Conolly had been put in charge of Hanwell asylum, which was the largest in the country, in 1839. He successfully abolished all forms of 'restraint' in the asylum, and argued that asylums were hospitals rather than prisons. Conolly's example led to the reform of many asylums.*

I From the *Report of the Visiting Justices of the Wandsworth County Asylum*, 1850:

> (There are) reasons to believe that, since the asylum ... opened, and the advantages it affords to lunatics have become known and recognized throughout the county, many poor insane persons, long previously neglected at home, have been brought to it.

J From *Practical Observations on Mental and Nervous Disorders*, by Alfred Beaumont Maddock, 1854:

> Unhappily ... disorders of the nervous system are no longer limited to the superior ranks of life, or to the idle and luxurious, but extensively co-exist, and have taken deep root, among the poorer as well as the middle orders of society.

K From the *Twelfth Report of the Poor Law Board*, 1858:

> ... we have been unable to discover any material changes in the social conditions of the labouring population rendering them more prone to mental disease ...

L *'A New Symbolical Head and Phrenological Chart.'* The idea that mental faculties were precisely located in specific areas of the brain became very fashionable for a while in the nineteenth century.

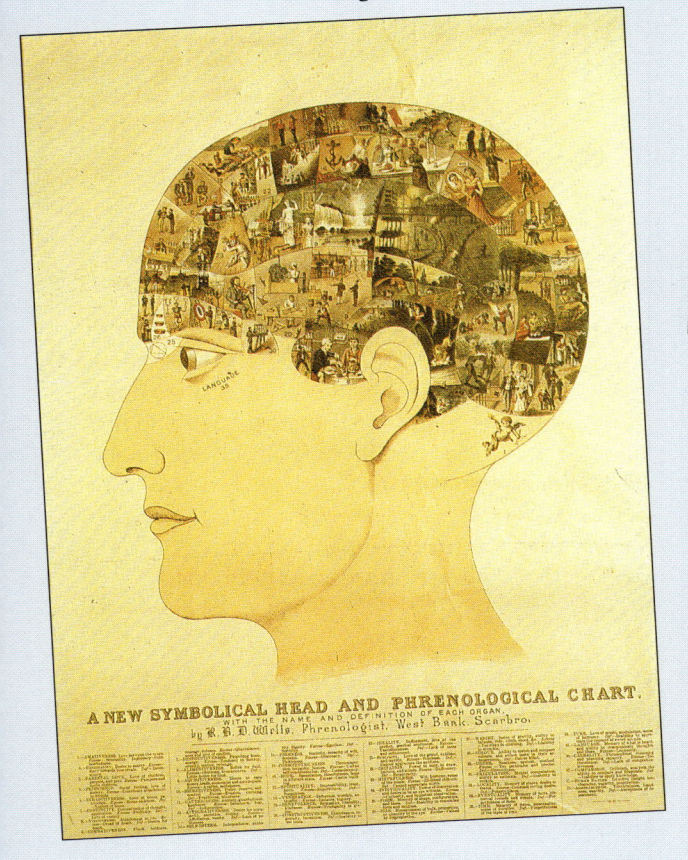

N From *The Times*, 5 April 1877:

> If lunacy continues to increase as at present, the insane will be in the majority, and, freeing themselves, will put the sane in asylums.

O Lord Shaftesbury speaking to the 1877 Select Committee:

> It must always be borne in mind ... that much is due to improved registration ... Since 1845 we are gradually becoming acquainted with the real state of lunacy in the country and I believe we have nearly got complete returns now.

Q From *The Rise of the Insane Asylum*, by Andrew Scull, 1975:

> ... The practical concerns of those running the asylum system were ... the isolation of those marginal elements of the population who could not or would not conform or could not subsist in an industrial ... society. The poor ... had little alternative but to make use of the asylum as a way of ridding themselves of what, in the circumstances of nineteenth century existence, was undoubtedly an intolerable burden, the caring for their sick, aged or otherwise incapacitated relatives.

P Photograph of the interior of a ward for female patients at the Prestwich Mental Hospital, Lancashire, around 1900.

M From the *Lunacy Annual Report* of 1861:

> There can be little doubt that the system of observation and inquiry adopted of late years, however imperfect it still may be, has led us to the detection and classification as Insane, of many persons formerly looked upon as ordinary paupers.

Questions
Using all the sources, explain what might have caused the increase in those people said to be suffering from mental illness during the nineteenth century.

Chapter 7 Florence Nightingale

An exercise in the analysis and evaluation of secondary sources

Florence Nightingale finds a place in every history of medicine and nursing. But the history books and biographies do not all tell the same story. This chapter looks at Florence Nightingale through these secondary sources.

A 'Florence Nightingale, an angel of mercy. Scutari Hospital, 1855', painting by Tomkins, 1855. Scutari Hospital was the main British military hospital during the Crimean War. Nightingale arrived at Scutari in 1854 with a small group of nurses.

B From *Florence Nightingale*, by Cecil Woodham-Smith, 1950:

It is possible to know a very great deal about Miss Nightingale's inner life and feelings because she had the habit of writing what she called 'private notes' ... She wrote them on anything that came to her hand – on odd pieces of blotting-paper, on the backs of calendars, the margins of letters ... it was in her private notes, written from girlhood to old age, that she recorded her true feelings, her secret experiences, and her uncensored opinions.

C From *A History of the Nursing Profession*, by Brian Abel-Smith, 1960:

Her own practical experience, combined with her own aims for the nursing profession, gave her a greater insight into the problems of hospital administration than her contemporaries, even in the medical profession. Her social position gave her a vantage point from which she could thrust her ideas on the committees that controlled the voluntary hospitals. But above all she had the determination to use every weapon she possessed, including charm, social pressure, and almost blackmail to achieve the objectives she had in mind. And by force of circumstance she became the greatest publicist the profession has ever had. Her adventures in the Crimea drew public attention on an enormous scale to the problems of nursing.

D *'One of the wards in the hospital at Scutari', painting by E. Walker after W. Simpson, 1856.*

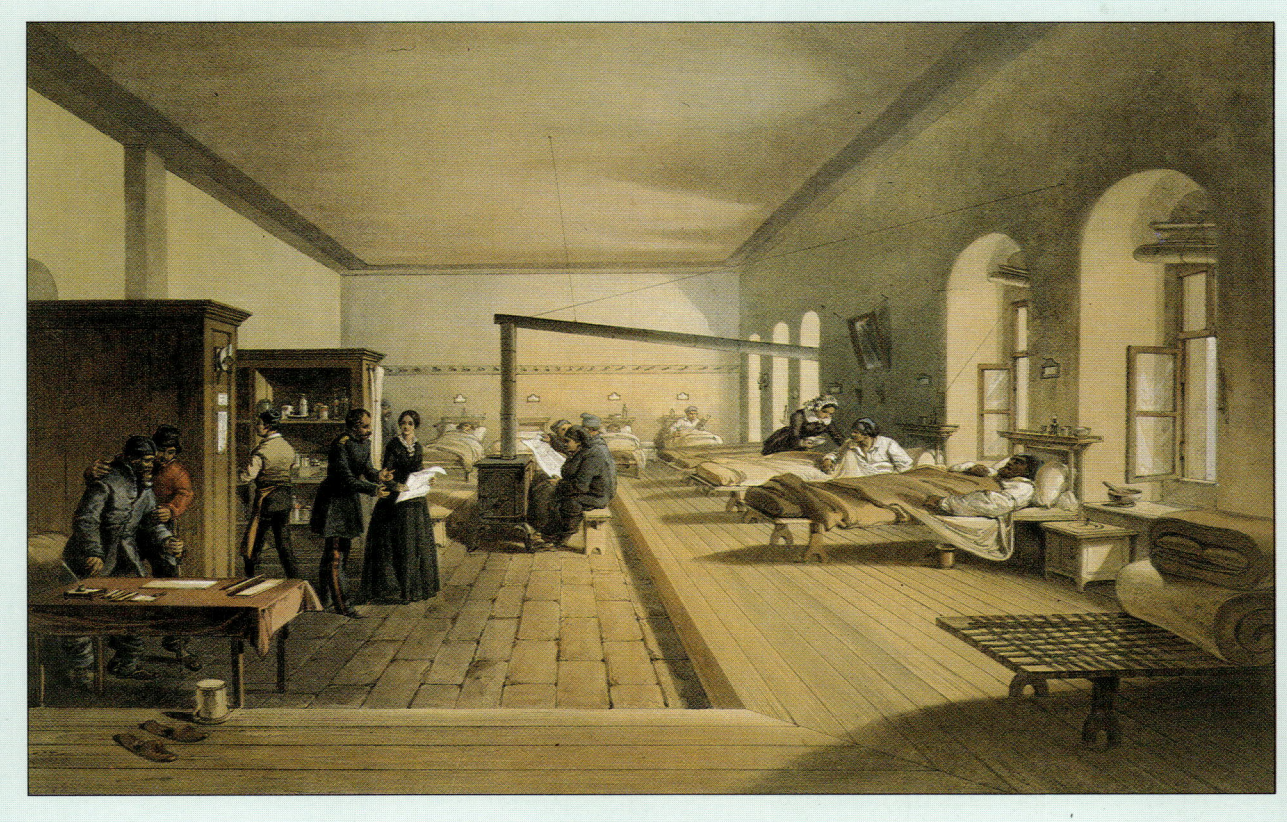

E *Photograph of Florence Nightingale shortly after her return from Crimea in 1856. On her return she began to plan reforms in nursing, in Army health care, hospitals and other matters.*

F From *A Short History of Nursing*, by Lavinia Dock, 1920:

The master plan (of Florence Nightingale's for a school of nursing) was brilliantly carried out ... the whole existing system of nursing in civil hospitals was revolutionised by the introduction into them of trained, refined women.

G From *The Nightingale Nurses: The Myth and the Reality*, by Monica Baly, 1987:

If we examine what the Nightingale School achieved in its early years, it is in fact very little ... Wherein, then, lay the success? The public relations machine is not new ... While Miss Nightingale was complaining that Mrs Wardroper (the nurse in charge of the School) was behaving like a 'semi-insane king' and the Nightingale Fund Council was wondering if it could move the school elsewhere, the experiment was being trumpeted in the general press and the medical journals as a great success. In history what people think is happening is often as important as what actually happened. The Nightingale fund was inundated for advice from other hospitals ... The publicity ... made nursing 'fashionable' and attracted recruits ...

H *Photograph taken in 1886 of Florence Nightingale at Claydon House, Oxfordshire.*

I From 'The nursing of the sick under Queen Victoria,' in the *British Medical Journal* in 1897:

... we must not forget that in the medical profession there was arising a demand for a higher class of women to tend at the bedside ... For in the 1830s ... the physician at the bedside and the surgeon in the operating theatre had the conviction forced upon them that if they were to do the best possible for their patients, they wanted hands, gentle, skilful, and sympathetic, which would work with them and for them ...

J *A ward in the London Hospital, 1888, from the* Illustrated London News, *1888.*

M From *An Introduction to the Social History of Nursing*, by R Dingwall, A Rafferty and C Webster, 1988:

The difficulty of assessing the contribution of Florence Nightingale to nursing reform in the nineteenth century is that so much of the writing about her has been biographical rather than historical. This has, perhaps, been encouraged by the mass of her own papers which present vivid, if often selective, melodramatic and egotistic accounts and judgements of other people and events. Florence Nightingale's life has taken on the function of a 'heroine legend' in nursing, a morality tale to inspire her successors. To see her, rather, as part of a social movement is not to detract from her contribution but is to acknowledge the complex relationship between individuals and their circumstances in the making of history.

K From *Eminent Victorians*, by Lytton Strachey, 1918:

With statesmen and governors at her beck and call, with her hands on a hundred strings, with mighty provinces at her feet, with foreign governments agog for her counsel, building hospitals, training nurses – she still felt that she had not enough to do. She sighed for more worlds to conquer – more, and yet more. She looked about her – what was there left? Of course! Philosphy! After the world of action, the world of thought. Having set right the health of the British Army, she would now do the same good service for the religious convictions of mankind ... Christianity itself was not without its defects. She would rectify these errors.

L From *Florence Nightingale: Reputation and Power*, by F. B. Smith, 1982:

In nursing, as in all her enterprises, Miss Nightingale's achievement was mixed. She gave nursing a public standing and independence within the medical hierarchy ... Her emphasis upon common sense care ... was invaluable ... but she added nothing to the details of technical proficiency required in a nurse's daily tasks. In workhouse nursing she had far-sighted ideas but she proved ready to abandon them for the immediate satisfaction of petty intrigues ... But then, she was less interested ... in general nursing ... than her contemporaries and later biographers have believed. Miss Nightingale served the cause of nursing less than it served her.

Questions

1 Read Source **M** carefully. How far do the other sources in the chapter support Source **M**? Illustrate your answer with reference to each source.   20

2 What have you learned from the sources about the advantages and disadvantages of relying on secondary sources in assessing the role of of Florence Nightingale?   10

Chapter 8 The reform of workhouse nursing

An exercise in interpretation of evidence

The workhouses created by the 1834 Poor Law Act were intended to deter the poor from being idle. But they soon began to fill with the sick poor, who had nowhere else to go. By the 1850s there were 50,000 sick people in the London workhouses alone, far more than in the voluntary hospitals. Medical care in these workhouse infirmaries was appalling, and the worst feature of it was the nursing. The nurses were themselves often pauper inmates, sometimes old or sick, often drunk or cruel, always untrained. Reform was essential but slow. The sources trace the path of reform from the 1840s to the 1900s.

A *'The Work-house Mrs Gamp', a cartoon from* Punch, *1866. The pauper nurse at the door is saying, 'Sorry to disturb you, Mum, but that child...'. The superintendent replies, 'Oh, bother the child! It's no use its being ill when I have a few friends to tea!'.*

B Two nurses – Sarah Gamp and Betsy Prig – portrayed in a scene from *Martin Chuzzlewit* by Charles Dickens, first published in 1844:

Mrs Gamp ascended to the sick-room, where her fellow-labourer Mrs Prig was dressing the invalid.

He was so wasted, that it seemed as if his bones would rattle when they moved him. His cheeks were sunken, and his eyes unnaturally large. He lay back in the easy chair like one more dead than living; and rolled his languid eyes towards the door where Mrs Gamp appeared, as painfully as if their weight alone were burdensome to move...

'Oh dear me!', cried the patient, 'oh dear, dear!'

'There!', said Mrs Prig, 'that's the way he's been conducting of himself, Sarah, ever since I got him out of bed, if you'll believe it'.

'Instead of being grateful', Mrs Gamp observed, 'for all our little ways. Oh, fie for shame, sir, fie for shame!'.

Here Mrs Prig seized the patient by the chin, and began to rasp his unhappy head with a hair-brush.

'I suppose you don't like that, neither!', she observed stopping to look at him.

It was just possible that he didn't, for the brush was a specimen of the hardest kind of instrument producible by modern art; and his very eyelids were red with the friction. Mrs Prig was gratified to observe the correctness of her supposition...

C Part of a letter from the Poor Law Board (which supervised the workhouse system) to Croydon Workhouse Infirmary in 1850, forbidding it to employ extra nurses:

> Three at least of the paid servants in this hospital must be discontinued. In the greater number of country unions (workhouses) there is no paid nurse and in none, it is believed, more than one ... The Poor Law Board attach more weight to the results of experience than to the opinion of the medical officer of the Croydon Workhouse, though supported by three of his professional friends.

D The reformer Louisa Twining began visiting workhouses in 1854 to gather information about their conditions. This is an entry from her diary in 1856.

> Went to see J. T. in the (workhouse). He was in a ward partly underground, with a stone floor; beds, sheets and shirts were dirty and grey. Said he had not seen the matron more than once during four months, only the chaplain and Guardians occasionally; nurse was an old R. C. (Roman Catholic), with bloated face, above 70. To get in I had to wait with a crowd at the office door to obtain a ticket. Visitors to the sick are only allowed once a week, for one hour.

E Florence Nightingale, writing in 1865 on the poor standards of nursing care in the workhouses:

> So long as a sick man, woman, or child is considered administratively to be a pauper, to be repressed, and not a fellow creature to be nursed into health, so long will these shameful disclosures have to be made.

F *'The Poor House or Pest House', lithograph from the 1850s.*

G 'Poor Laws: as they were; as they are', a cartoon from the early nineteenth century suggesting that Poor Law authorities were being extravagant.

H 'New Workhouse for the Parishes of Fulham and Hammersmith', feature in the Illustrated London News of August 1849.

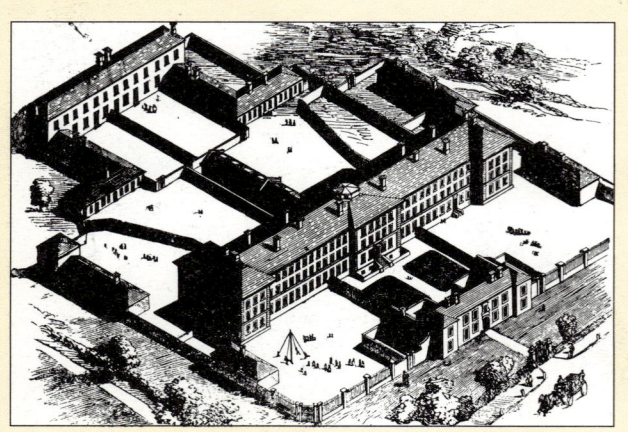

I Cartoon from 1880 showing the reaction of hard-hearted guardians to a starving man.

First Guardian (to Second). "Oh, by the way, saw a very curious sight coming along—fellow actually dying of starvation on the pavement; very interesting thing to see."

J In 1865 the medical journal *The Lancet* launched a campaign to reform the workhouses:

> ... the general character of the nursing will be appreciated by the details of the one fact, that we found in one ward two paralytic patients with frightful sloughs of the back; they were both dirty and lying on hard straw mattresses – the one dressed only with a rag steeped in chloride of lime solution, the other with a rag thickly covered with ointment ... the stench was masked by strewing dry chloride of lime on the floor under the bed ... Both these patients have since died; no inquest has been held on either.
> ... The workhouse hospitals sin by their own construction, by their want of nursing, by their comfortless fittings, by the supremacy which is accorded to the question of expense ... This state of things cannot continue. It is necessary that public opinion should be fully enlightened and deliberately directed.

sloughs = sores

K Matilda Beeton was a nurse at the Rotherhithe Workhouse Infirmary when it was visited by inspectors checking the claims of the *Lancet*. She wrote to them afterwards.

> I well remember, sir, your visit to the Rotherhithe Infirmary, the Master accompanied you. I answered yes when I ought to have said no; this I did fearing the Master or Matron would hear me or you would tell them, and then I might be reported, and that is anything but pleasant ... This rod was shook over me, sir.

L Part of a letter from Florence Nightingale in 1867:

> The whole reform in nursing both at home and abroad has consisted in this; to take all power over the Nursing out of the hands of the men, and put it into the hands of one female trained head and make her responsible for everything (regarding internal management and discipline) being carried out.

M From 'Workhouse Infirmaries', in *Macmillan's Magazine*, July 1881:

> Pauper women are selected for nursing by the matron, and all the pay they receive is some beer, and occasionally a half-a-crown a week. The master observes that he can manage this sort of woman much better than trained nurses, as they are wholly dependent on his will, and his power over them is despotic.

N When the *Report of the Royal Commission on the Poor Laws* was published in 1909, it contained masses of evidence on nursing in the workhouse infirmaries. In the urban infirmaries it reported that there were too few nurses but that standards seemed to be high. In the rural workhouses, it stated, many infirmaries had problems in recruiting nurses because of low pay, poor accommodation, long hours, and boring work:

> ... there are still many rural workhouses without even one trained nurse; there are still scores in which there is absolutely no nurse, trained or untrained, available for night duty; there are even some, so far as we can ascertain, in which there is no sort of salaried nurse at all. Everywhere the Master and Matron have still to employ pauper assistants to help in attending the sick.

O 'Fifty Years, 1838–1888', an illustration from the Nursing Record, 1888.

P Photograph of meal-time at the Marylebone Workhouse, taken around 1900.

Questions

1. Examine Sources **A** and **O**, and read Source **B**. What do they suggest about the attitude and standards of nurses in the early nineteenth century? 6
2. Refer to Sources **C**, **D** and **G**, **H**, **I**, **J**, and **K**. Why, according to these sources, was the quality of nursing in workhouse infirmaries so poor? 12
3. Using Sources **L**, **M**, **N**, **O**, and **P**, describe progress in nursing reform over the period covered. 12

Chapter 9 Safer surgery

An exercise in the analysis of historical narrative

This chapter examines the development of surgery during the nineteenth century. The main source in the chapter is a historical narrative taken from *The Development of Modern Medicine*, by the medical historian Richard Shryock.

A *A modern reconstruction of what naval surgery would have been like around 1800.*

B *A watercolour showing surgery in the home. It has the inscription 'R Power, operated on July 28th, Died this Aug 11th. 1817'.*

C From *The Development of Modern Medicine*, by Richard Shryock, 1948:

So long as disease had been thought of as a vague state of the body fluids ... there was no incentive to operate save as a last resort in obvious emergencies. One cannot, after all, operate on the blood. But once diseases were traced to lesions in specific organs, the most immediate way to deal with them was to remove the diseased parts wherever possible. The growing scepticism about internal medicine made surgery seem even more desirable, simply because there seemed to be no alternative ...

The contrast involved can be observed in the case of appendicitis. In 1800, or even in 1850, acute pain in the lower right side was likely to be treated by purging, and as a last resort by morphine. Here the hand of the physician was still guided by ancient humoral conceptions, which naturally did not suggest surgical interference. The local pathology of appendicitis was described early in the century, however, and clear cases of rupture were subsequently found at autopsy. To prevent this development, Henry Hancock of London first removed an appendix in 1848. A generation thereafter the operation was gradually adopted as a regular procedure.

The surgeon was here taking the place, it will be noted, of the general practitioner ... Under these circumstances an increasing interest was naturally displayed in improving all the techniques and procedures of his art. This interest had appeared before 1800, but grew faster after 1840. The discoveries that followed may be viewed as the effects rather than – as is usually assumed – the cause of the modern emphasis on surgery ...

One of the basic difficulties in most operations

was that of the patient's suffering, since this encouraged haste on the part of the surgeon. Any means of avoiding pain would obviously aid the latter by enabling him to proceed deliberately and without distractions. It must also be remembered that even hardened surgeons had human qualities, and those who worked during the 1840s were doubtless influenced in some degree by the rising humanitarianism of the times ... In a word, surgeons had both technical and moral reasons for seeking a victory over pain.

... dentists were probably under greater pressure than surgeons to find some means for preventing pain. The latter usually served a patient only once. and then in a case of dire necessity. But dentists saw their patients recurrently, and must persuade them to accept treatments that were not absolutely necessary. If painless work could be assured, patients would accept further treatments, and professional opportunities would expand to the benefit of the public as well as of the dentists.

These circumstances, combined with the availability of such chemicals as ether and chloroform, may explain the sporadic experiments with anaesthesia made ... between 1825 and 1845 ... lecturers introduced ether inhalations as a popular amusement. In the course of one of these 'ether parties' Dr Crawford W. Long of Georgia accidentally noted the effects of the gas in preventing pain. He thereupon successfully used it as an anaesthetic during several operations in 1842; but, fearful of public censure for using a dangerous procedure, made no reports.

In 1844 Horace Wells, of Hartford, Connecticut, impressed by a popular demonstration of the effects of nitrous oxide, began using that gas in dental work; but a fatal case caused him to withdraw from practice. It remained for another dentist to whom Wells had transmitted his ideas, W. T. G. Morton, to return to the use of ether. Morton persuaded Dr J. C. Warren to permit a famous demonstration in the Massachusetts General Hospital in 1846, which definitely introduced the use of ether into surgical practice in both America and Europe.

Once the inhalation of ether was accepted as a desirable means for producing anaesthesia, there was naturally an interest in experimenting with other gases for the same purpose. In 1847 Sir James Simpson of Edinburgh introduced the use of chloroform into surgical procedure. This gas was easier to use than ether, and soon became the more popular, and remained so until almost 1900.

It was obvious that anaesthesia was a major contribution to human welfare, and also of great technical advantage to surgeons. The latter were now free to try procedures which had hitherto been beyond them ... In the long run the new freedom did much to revolutionize surgery. (But) there was some danger here in the pre-antiseptic decades, since surgical interference was now made easier, and so increased the risks from infection.

Wound infections had always been the chief cause of the mortality following operations of any sort ... The English surgeon John Bell stated, in 1812, that abdominal wounds were so dangerous that it was only necessary to record the rare cases of recovery. Compound fractures were so commonly fatal that amputation was usually resorted to, but the latter procedure itself represented only a choice of evils ... Of the 13,000 amputations performed by French army surgeons during the Franco-Prussian War (1870), no fewer than 10,000 proved fatal!

... Here and there individual surgeons were greatly concerned about the whole situation; and some attempted unsuccessfully to lessen mortality by cleanliness and by the employment of special washes for wounds ... Pasteur's demonstration that bacteria were responsible for fermentations now gave the clue that was needed to reform surgical procedure all along the line.

Joseph Lister, who had been seeking for three years to reduce the mortality in the surgical wards of the Glasgow Infirmary, seized upon this clue in 1864 and put it to a systematic test. If microorganisms caused wound fermentation (suppuration) they must be excluded at all costs. Not only the hands and instruments of the surgeon must be clean, but the very air surrounding the patient must be purified. Searching for a powerful antiseptic, Lister followed the sanitarians in adopting carbolic acid, and provided a continuous spray of this over the wound during operation. It was immediately found that this prevented infection and permitted healing in the majority of cases. Experience later showed the air-spray to be unnecessary; but this is no way changed the principles involved ... The work of the British surgeon eventually made a great impression on the entire Western world ... Surgery was at last rendered relatively safe as well as relatively painless. This development, in combination with the continued use of anaesthetics, made possible many types of operations hitherto unthinkable. An ancient but very limited art was metamorphosed, within a generation, into a potent and impressive science. The development of antiseptic surgery was, then, one of the first triumphs of modern medicine.

lesions = changes caused by disease
humoral conceptions = theories which explained diseases in terms of imbalances of body fluids such as blood, bile and phlegm. These humoral theories were probably Greek in origin, and lasted until the early nineteenth century
pathology = symptoms of disease
anaesthesia = a loss of the powers of feeling
censure = disapproval
metamorphosed = changed

D *A painting by Ernest Board showing the first use of ether in dental surgery, by William Morton, in 1846.*

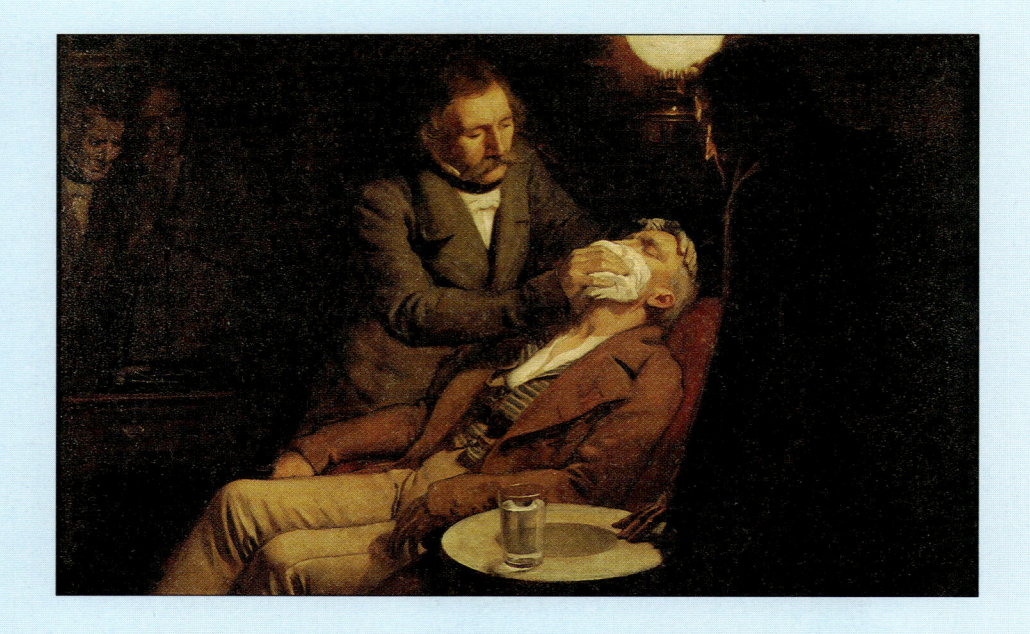

E *Drawing of Simpson and his colleagues discovering the effects of chloroform.*

F *Joseph Lister's comparison of amputations done between 1864 and 1866 without using carbolic acid, with those done using carbolic acid between 1867 and 1869.*

Year	Number of amputations	Number of patients	
		Recovered	Died
1864–1866	35	19	16
1867–1869	40	34	6

G *Engraving showing carbolic spray being used during an operation around 1870.*

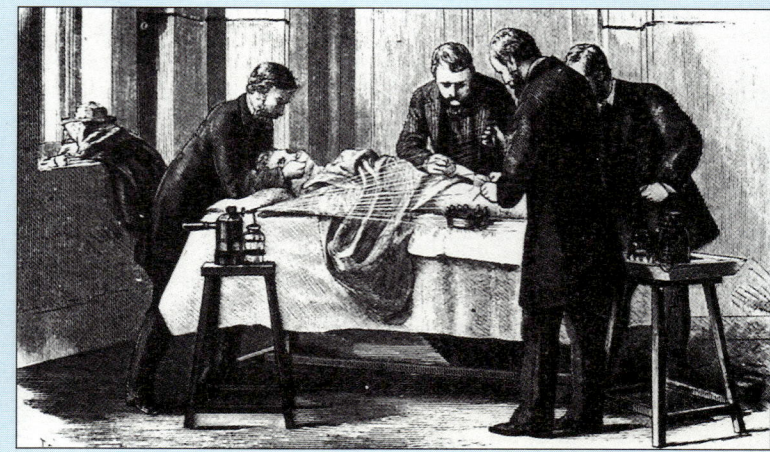

40

H *Photograph of Lister and his staff in King's College Medical School, in 1893.*

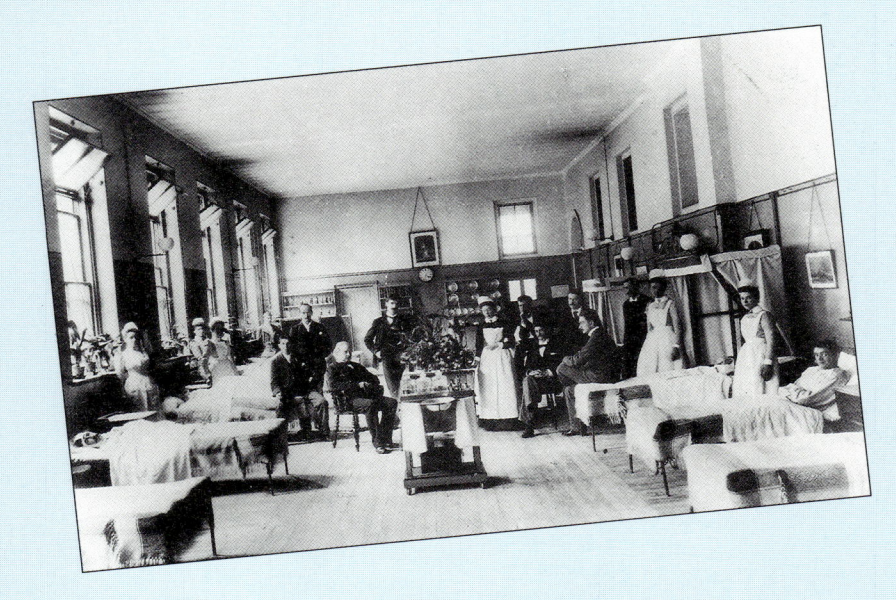

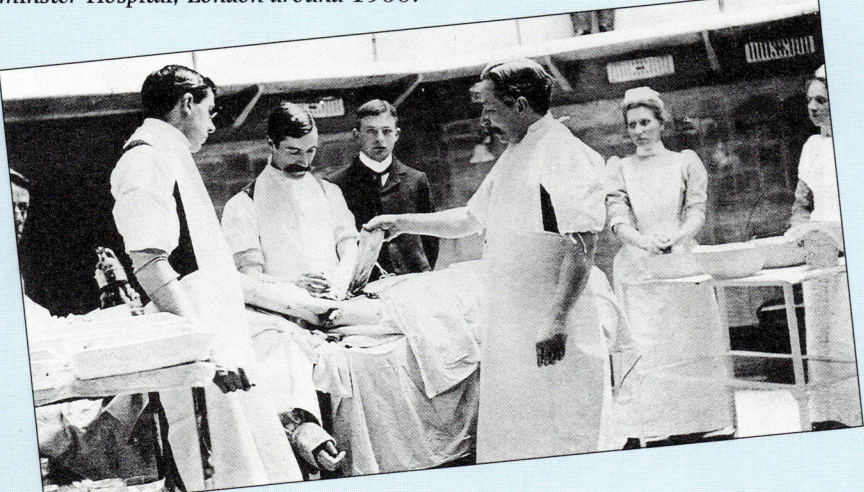

'An Advanced Dressing Station at the front', painted in 1922 by Henry Tonks. Army surgeons sort the wounded into groups so that those needing immediate surgery will not have to wait.

I *Photograph showing a surgical operation being performed by W.G. Spencer and others at the Westminster Hospital, London around 1900.*

Questions
1 Refer to Sources **A**, **B**, and **C**.
   a What was surgery like before the introduction of anaesthetics and antiseptic methods? 4
   b What effect did the introduction of anaesthetics have on surgery in the period before antiseptic methods were introduced? 4
2 Why does Shryock claim that surgical discoveries were an effect rather than a cause of the modern emphasis on surgery? Use evidence from Source **C** to support your answer. 6
3 What, according to Shryock, were the main reasons behind the search for an anaesthetic, and in what way do these reasons help to explain who first introduced anesthetics? 6
4 Using Sources **C** and **F**, **G**, **H**, and **I**, explain in your own words the contribution of Joseph Lister to the development of surgery. 10

41

Chapter 10 Penicillin – Fleming and Florey

An exercise in historical judgement

This chapter is about two scientists: Alexander Fleming and Howard Florey. Although Fleming discovered the antibiotic penicillin, it was Florey who went on to demonstrate how valuable penicillin could be in treating humans. However, Fleming rather than Florey became world famous.

A *Alexander Fleming's photograph of his original culture plates, taken in 1928. Fleming's discovery of penicillin in 1928 in his laboratory at St Mary's Hospital, London, is one of the most famous events in medical science. Fleming noticed that some mould had grown in a culture plate of germs, killing the germs. Fleming studied the mould and noted that it prevented a number of bacteria from growing. He named it penicillin.*

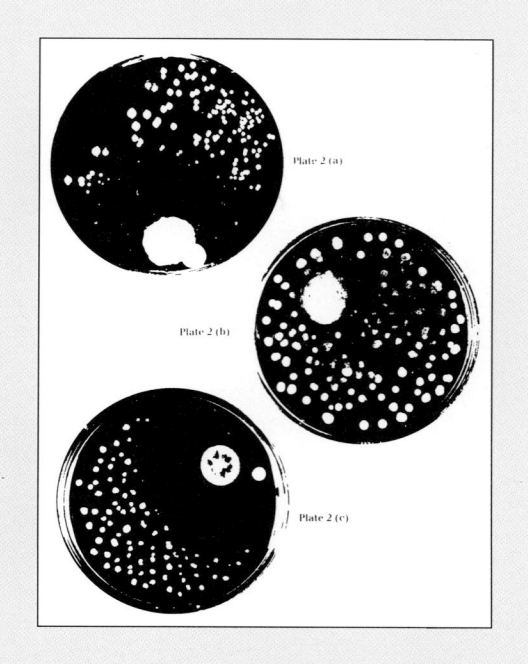

B From *Alexander Fleming: the Man and the Myth*, by Gwyn Macfarlane, 1984:

No one to whom Fleming showed his mouldy culture plate on that September morning in 1928 realized that they were looking at something that would eventually revolutionize the practice of medicine. What they saw, when Fleming pointed it out to them, was that it was covered with the recognizable colonies of staphylococci, except in the vicinity of a growth of mould near the edge of the plate, In this area the colonies were ghost-like and transparent, and quite close to the mould there were none at all ... it was only some fifteen years later, when the truly historic importance of the episode became apparent, that the first eye-witnesses tried to recall precisely what had happened.

staphyloccocus = a type of bacteria

C From a speech by Alexander Fleming to the American Pharmaceutical Manufacturers' Association, December 1943:

From 1930 to 1939 I expect that my laboratory at St Mary's Hospital was the only one where penicillin was in constant use, not for the treatment of patients, but for the isolation of certain microbes – a minor use, but not without value.

D In 1938 a group of scientists at Oxford, led by Howard Florey, started research on penicillin, and by 1940 they were ready to test its effect by an experiment on eight mice. This account is from *Howard Florey: the Making of a Great Scientist*, By Gwyn Macfarlane, 1979:

On the morning of Saturday 25th May 1940, Florey did the experiment. This is the day, surely, that does mark one of the historic turning-points in medical history ... Eight lethal doses (of streptococci bacteria) were prepared and waiting. At 11 a.m. Florey ... injected each of the eight mice ... with the dose of ... streptococci. Four of the mice he put back into their cages without further treatment ... (The other four were treated with injections of varying amounts of penicillin to counter the effects of the streptococci) ... Next morning, Sunday 26 May, Florey came into the department to discover that the results of his experiment were clear-cut indeed. All four control mice were dead. Three of the treated mice were perfectly well; the fourth was not so well – though it survived for another two days. (The scientists) all recognized that this was a momentous occasion.

Chart showing the experiment on eight mice in Oxford on 25 May 1940. The chart is based on a drawing by one of the scientists involved, Dr N. G. Heatley. Eight mice were infected with an injection of streptococci. Four mice were then given doses of penicillin. The chart shows how long each mouse survived.

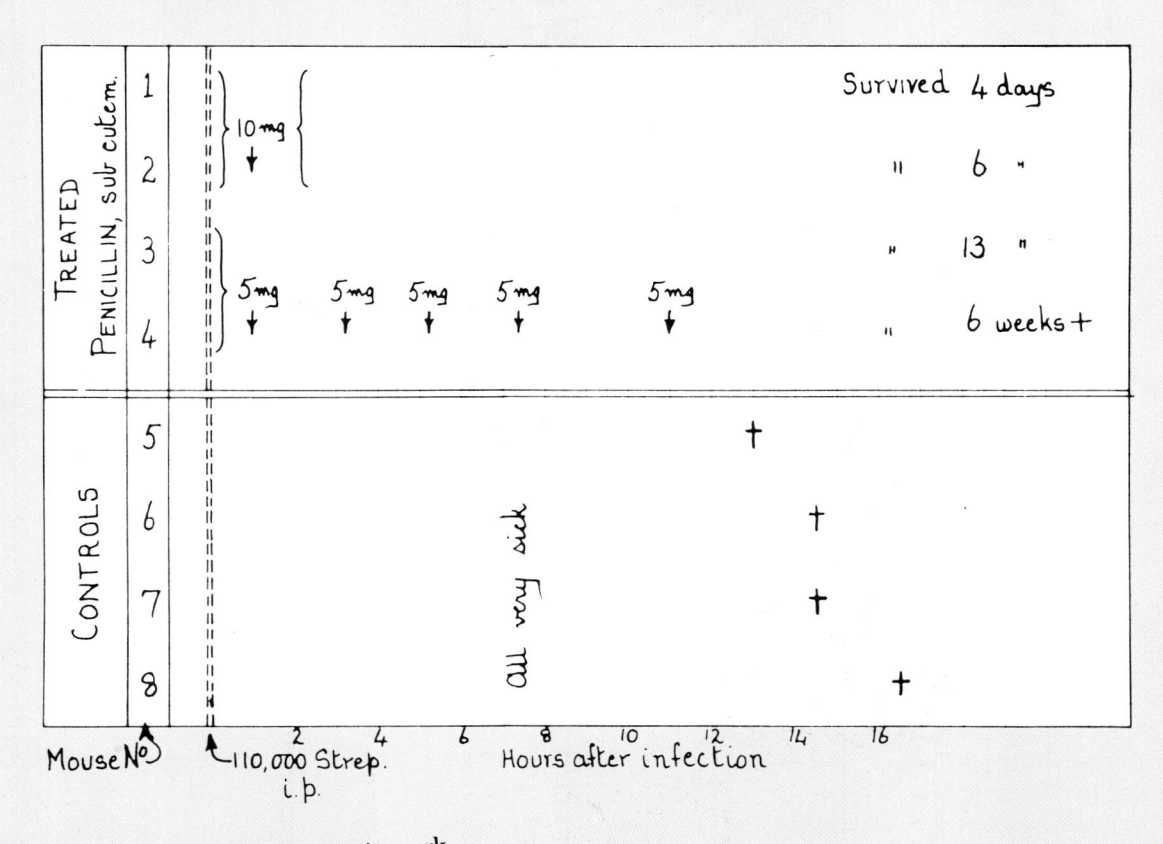

E On 24 August 1940 the Oxford team's work showing the effect of penicillin on mice was published in *The Lancet*. A few days later Fleming phoned up to say he'd like to visit. Florey told his colleague Ernst Chain that Fleming was coming. Chain replied:

Fleming? Good God; I thought he was dead.

F *Photograph of penicillin being made in ceramic 'bed-pans' at the William Dunn School of Pathology, University of Oxford, sometime in 1940 or 1941. The Oxford scientists had at first used real bed-pans in which to produce penicillin, as they were a good shape and size for growing mould. Eventually a Midlands pottery made the ceramic containers shown here.*

G From *Penicillin in Perspective*, by D. Wilson, 1976:

The scientists of Oxford University (Florey and Chain) made four quite crucial achievements which together amounted to giving the world the first antibiotic: penicillin. Their four achievements:
1) to show that penicillin was a usable clinical drug with powers of curing infection that were beyond the wildest dreams of man ...
2) to isolate and purify penicillin to a state in which it could safely be used for human patients.
3) They carried out the first clinical testing of penicillin on humans ...
4) They found out how to manufacture penicillin on a commercial scale.

H *Photograph of Sir Howard Florey in 1962. Florey received many awards: he was knighted in 1944, shared a Nobel prize with Fleming and Chain in 1954, and in 1960 was elected President of the Royal Society, the highest honour that a scientist can be awarded in Britain. But he never became a household name in the way Fleming did.*

I Florey, speaking to the Royal Society of Arts, London, 10 November 1944:

> In 1940, the first observations on penicillin were published ... up to this time the real nature of penicillin had escaped detection.

J Sir Almroth Wright, Head of Fleming's Inoculation Department in St Mary's Hospital, in a letter to *The Times*, 30 August 1942:

> Sir: In the leading article on penicillin in your article yesterday you refrained from putting the laurel wreath for this discovery round anybody's brow. I would, with your permission, supplement your article by pointing out that ... it should be decreed to Professor Alexander Fleming of this laboratory. For he is the discoverer of penicillin and was the author also of the original suggestion that this substance might prove to have important applications in medicine.

K Florey to his colleague N.G. Heatley, in late summer of 1942:

> I fear disruption to our work and to my schedule and I hate getting involved in committees. But, more than all this, it is utterly wrong to write about this drug as 'magic'. It is not a cure-all and it is cruel to raise hope among the dying and their relatives that such a substance exists and then to tell them that they cannot have it supplied.

L Florey said to his secretary on arrival of the press at the laboratories in Oxford in September 1942:

> ... send them packing. I won't talk to them now. Tell them to come back next Thursday and I may give them ten minutes.

M From *Memoir of Lord Florey*, by Professor E. P. Abraham, 1971:

> The press sent representatives [to Florey in Oxford] who received no welcome and little satisfaction from their visit ... one result ... was that the press went where it was not rebuffed and published accounts of penicillin which were tendentious and one-sided ...

tendentious = leaning or tending towards one side

N Ernst Chain, on the story being leaked to the press in 1942:

> The British hospitals were struggling for their pennies, remember. Then, here suddenly, was a pot of gold for St Mary's. It was an opportunity to be grasped – and, if I had been manager of the hospital, I might have done the same thing.

O From a letter from Florey to Sir Henry Dale, President of the Royal Society, December 1942:

> As you know, there has been a lot of most undesirable publicity in the newspapers and press generally about penicillin ... the whole subject is presented as having been foreseen and worked out by Fleming. ... This steady propaganda seems to be having its effect even on scientific people, in that several have now said to us 'But I thought you had done something on penicillin too'.

P Photograph of Sir Alexander Fleming being installed as Rector of the University of Edinburgh in 1952.

Q Because penicillin saved the lives of many matadors gored by bulls, the matadors of Barcelona erected this statue in honour of Alexander Fleming.

R From *Alexander Fleming: the Man and the Myth*, by Gwyn Macfarlane, 1984:

Fleming's reaction to public mis-statements about himself was an amused detachment. He made no attempt to deny or correct them. Indeed he positively enjoyed them ... He carefully preserved the cuttings in a book labelled 'Fleming Myth', enjoyed retailing them to his friends, and might even pin up the choicest examples on the departmental notice board.

S From Florey to Sir Edward Mellanby, Secretary of the Medical Research Council, on 19 June 1944:

It has long been a source of irritation to us all here to witness the unscrupulous campaign carried on from St Mary's calmly to credit Fleming with all the work done here ... My policy here has been never to interview the press or allow them to get any information from us even by telephone ... In contrast, Fleming has been interviewed apparently without cease, photographed etc. ... with the upshot that he is being put over as 'the discoverer of penicillin' (which is true) with the implication that he did all the work leading to the discovery of its chemotherapeutic properties (which is not true) ... my colleagues here feel things are going much too far.

chemotherapeutic = treatment of diseases by chemical substances.

T From Sir Edward Mellanby to Florey, 30 June 1944:

... scientific men ... know that, from the point of view of scientific merit, your work and that of your colleagues stands on a much higher level than that of Fleming. ... If you are at all affected by what appears in the public press, you can be quite certain that this is an ephemeral reaction which means little or nothing ... In time, even the public will realise that in the development of this story of penicillin the thing that has mattered most has been the persistent and highly meritorious work of your laboratory.

U From *Howard Florey: the Making of a Great Scientist*, by Gwyn Macfarlane, 1979:

The Fleming Myth ... will probably survive any efforts to establish the truth ... because a popular myth is one of the most indestructible things on earth.

Modern photograph of penicillin being manufactured.

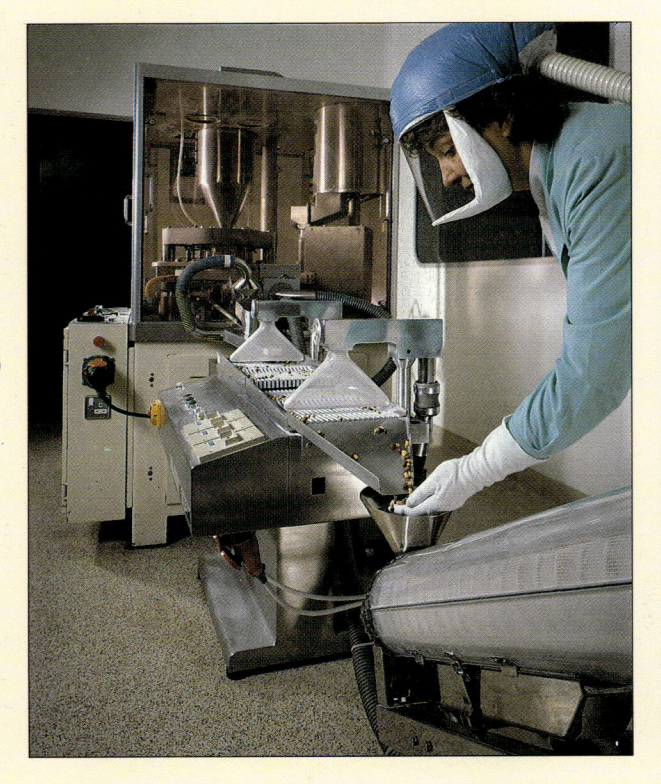

Questions

1. Study Sources **A**, **B**, **C**, **D**, **E**, **F**, and **G**. What part in the story of penicillin was played by:
    a) Fleming?
    b) Florey and his colleagues?   10
2. Use Sources **J**, **K**, **L**, **M**, **N**, **R**, and **S** to explain why Fleming gained most of the public credit for penicillin while the work of Florey and his colleagues was not widely appreciated.   10
3. a) Read Source **U**. In your opinion, and drawing on the other sources in the chapter, which parts of the story of Fleming does Macfarlane consider a 'myth'?
    b) In your opinion, does the story of penicillin support Macfarlane's views in Source **U** about popular myths?   4

Chapter 11 The creation of the National Health Service

An exercise in the use of cartoons as historical evidence

William Beveridge, a civil servant, had been asked by Britain's wartime government to prepare plans for Britain's future social services. His report was published in December 1942. It went much further than anyone had expected, proposing a comprehensive system of social security, guaranteed full employment, and a national health service. The government was alarmed at the cost of the proposals, but the public greeted them with great enthusiasm.

This chapter looks at the origins and early years of the National Health Service through the eyes of newspaper cartoonists. Study them carefully, then answer the questions.

B *Cartoon from the* Daily Express, *17 February 1943.*

A *Cartoon by David Low, Evening Standard, 3 December 1942. In the bus is a character with a walrus moustache. He was called Colonel Blimp. David Low invented the Colonel before the Second World War as a symbol of the backward-looking person in charge.*

C *Cartoon by David Low, Evening Standard, 8 March 1943. After the First World War politicians had promised 'to make Britain a fit country for heroes to live in', but instead there had been a depression and mass unemployment.*

47

D From *The Audit of War*, By Corelli Barnett, 1986:

... from the moment when the Conservative-dominated coalition government so tepidly greeted the Beveridge Plan at the beginning of 1943, the nation ... had come more and more to the conclusion that what stood between it and the Better Britain of its dreams was 'them', 'the old gang', the political leadership of the 1930s which in its meanness over expenditure and its lack of bold imagination had done nothing about unemployment or poverty before the war ...

E *Cartoon by David Low*, Evening Standard, 2 August 1943.

F *Cartoon by David Low*, Evening Standard, 26 June 1944.

G The results of the 1935 and 1945 General Elections showing the number of MPs elected.

Party	Year 1935	Year 1945
Labour	154	393
Conservative	432	213
Liberal	20	12

H *'Not so much of that "cradle to the grave" stuff, young 'Erbert. Grandpa's sensitive'*, by Joe Lee, Evening News, 5 October 1944. *'From the cradle to the grave' was a phrase used to indicate the completeness of Beveridge's proposals, which included maternity grants and funeral grants.*

I From *The People's War*, by Angus Calder, 1969:

The chief dissenters (to the National Health Service proposed by the Government in a White Paper in 1944) were the leaders of the British Medical Association, who tried frantically to discredit it ... the BMA kept up an unedifying racket until the very eve of the new service's creation.

J Cartoon by David Low, Evening Standard, 14 December 1944. Charles Hill, shown praying at the foot of the bed, was the Secretary of the British Medical Association (the main doctors' union). He led the opposition to the National Health Service.

K Cartoon by David Low, Evening Standard, 15 January 1948. Charles Hill dreams of Aneurin Bevan on the operating table. Bevan was the Minister for Health in the Labour Government after 1945, and it was his job to steer the National Health Service into existence.

L 'Doctors v. Bevan: Hm! You'll have to take things more gently and on no account get excited', cartoon by Joe Lee, Evening News, 19 February 1948.

M 'D-Day: Take him away! Doctor Bevan can't deal with him personally even if he HAS got the best collection of ailments in London', cartoon by Joe Lee, Evening News, 1 July 1948. July 5 1948 was the 'Appointed Day' on which the National Health Service came into existence.

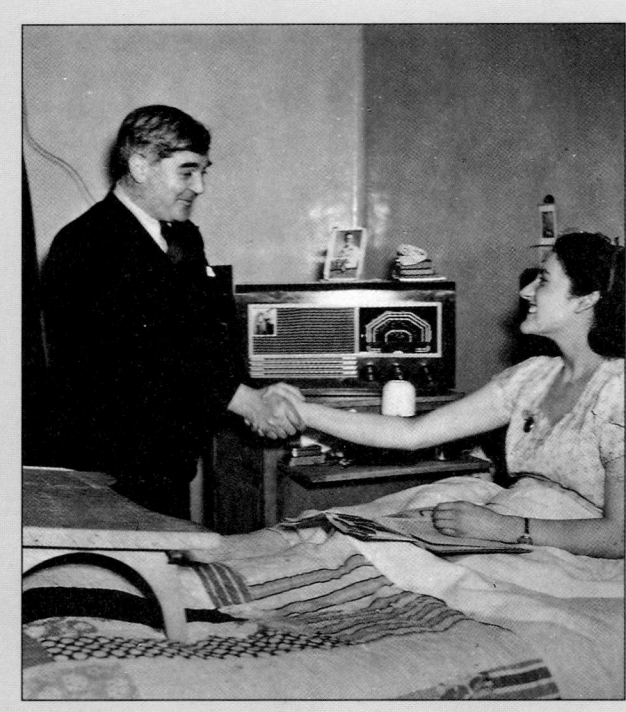

Aneurin Bevan, Minister of Health, visiting Papworth Village Hospital in May 1948.

N 'Doctor's manner changes with NHS: Has anyone noticed any difference in that doctor's bedside manners now we're on the panel', cartoon by Joe Lee, Evening News, *12 July 1948*. The National Health Service gave doctors a fee for each patient on their list or 'panel', so there was less incentive for them to spend much time with their patients.

O 'They're no better. I can still read the news', cartoon by Joe Lee, Evening News, *7 October, 1948*. When the National Health Service began, spectacles were free of charge, but charges were introduced in 1950.

50

P *Cartoon by David Low, Evening Standard, 9 December 1948. The National Health Service paid dentists a fee for each treatment they provided, and this let some dentists earn large amounts of money in the early days of the Service.*

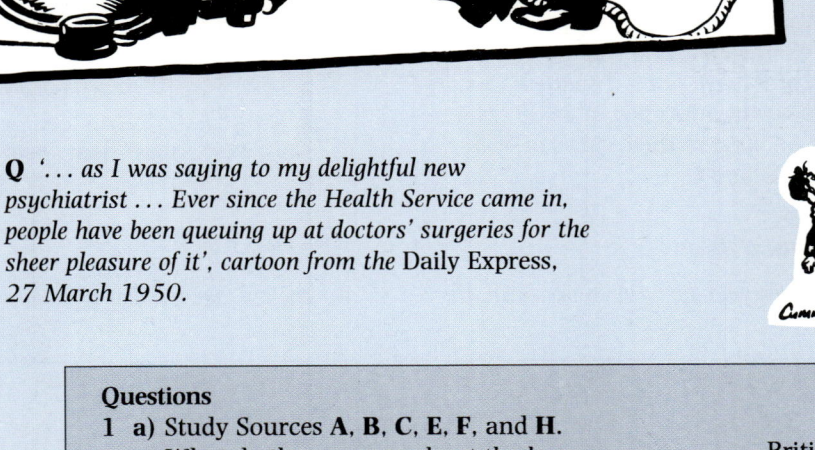

"OPEN WIDE, PLEASE. I'M AFRAID THIS MIGHT HURT A LITTLE"

Q *'... as I was saying to my delightful new psychiatrist ... Ever since the Health Service came in, people have been queuing up at doctors' surgeries for the sheer pleasure of it', cartoon from the Daily Express, 27 March 1950.*

R *'Doctor Rising Price', cartoon from the Daily Express, 29 June 1958. Critics of the National Health Service claimed it was expensive, but an official enquiry published in 1956 proved that it cost far less than most people suspected and was good value.*

Questions

1. **a)** Study Sources **A**, **B**, **C**, **E**, **F**, and **H**. What do they convey about the hopes and fears raised by the Beveridge Report? — 6

   b) Read Source **D** and study Source **G**. How far do these Sources support Sources **A**, **B**, **C**, **E**, **F**, and **H**? Refer to the cartoons when answering the question. — 4

2. Read Source **I** and study the cartoons Sources **J**, **K**, and **L**. Referring to each cartoon in turn, explain the attitude expressed in the cartoon towards the British Medical Association and the negotiations between the government and the doctors. — 6

3. Study the cartoons Sources **M**, **N**, **O**, **P**, **Q**, and **R**. What attitude towards the National Health Service is expressed in each of the cartoons? — 8

4. Of what value are these cartoons in studying of the National Health Service? Support your answer by referring to the cartoons. — 6

51

Chapter 12 Women and childbirth

A study in the use of oral history as historical evidence

This chapter examines the changing experience of women as mothers this century. As the graphs in Source **A** show, there have been some dramatic changes in the dangers of childbirth to mother and baby, and in the average number of children that women give birth to. Almost all the remaining sources in the chapter explore these changes by means of *oral history*: people talking about their own lives in their own words. Most of the sources come from two books based on recorded interviews with people: *A Woman's Place: An Oral History of Working-Class Women 1890–1940*, by Elizabeth Roberts published in 1984, and *Out of the Doll's House: The Story of Women in the Twentieth Century*, by Angela Holdsworth, published in 1988. The authors of these books give their views of oral history in Sources **B** and **C**.

A *Three graphs showing statistics for England and Wales.*

i) *The infant mortality rate (the proportion of babies who die at birth or within the first year of life) from 1881 to 1981*

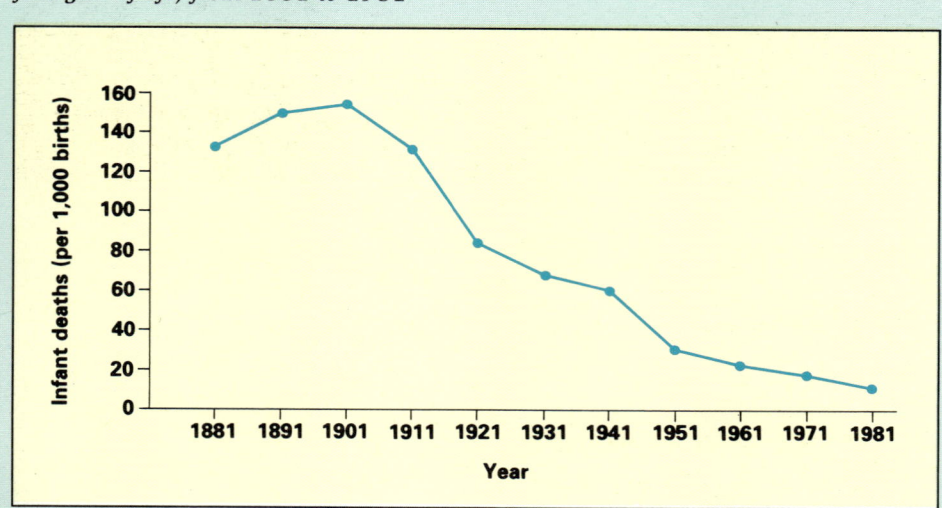

ii) *The maternal mortality rate (the proportion of births in which the mother died) from 1881 to 1981*

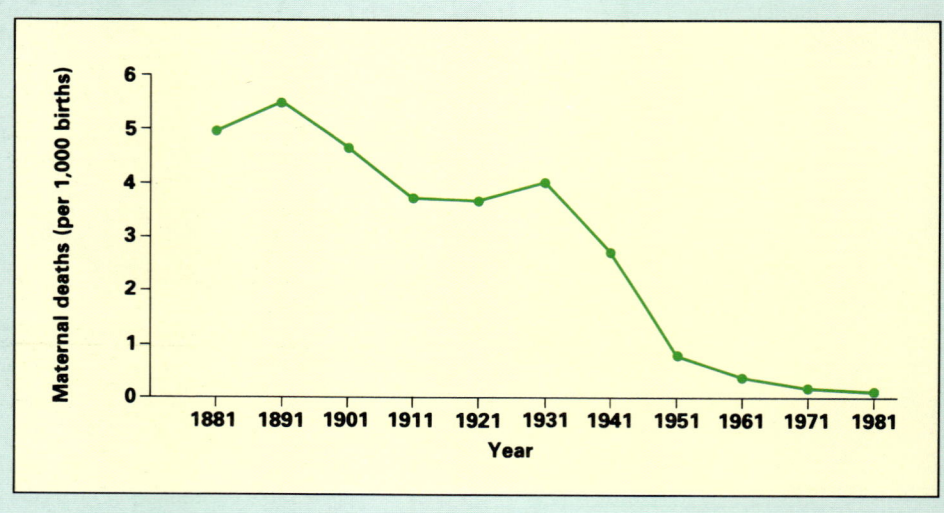

iii) *The average number of children born to married couples from 1870 to 1975.*

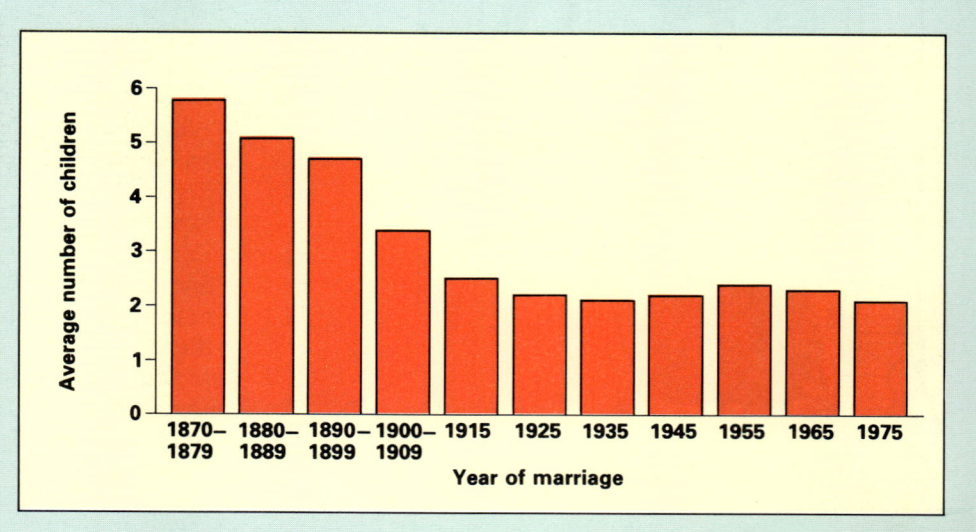

B From *A Woman's Place*:

... working-class people ... were and are less likely to keep diaries, write letters, or enter items in account books than their more prosperous, educated and leisured contemporaries. In the absence of this personal documentary evidence, oral evidence is vital. Through old people's spoken testimony about their lives and those of their parents, one can attempt to reconstruct a picture of everyday life over the last century.

C From *Out of the Doll's House*:

The span of living memory dictated we should start our story around the beginning of the century. Our research was drawn from the personal recollections of a wide variety of people, ranging in age from 18 to 102 ... Together they provide a snapshot view of history, a picture of the past brought to life by reminiscences.

D From *A Woman's Place*. Mrs Mitchell was born in 1913. She was one of six children. Her mother was 46 when Mrs Mitchell was born. Here she is asked why her mother's generation often had such large families:

In those days there was no birth control. They took the risk you see. If it happened, it happened. That's why they had such big families ... There's no need for a big family, they have a choice these days, but in those days they hadn't.

E *Photograph of Mr and Mrs Terry of Greenwich, taken in 1914, with some of their 19 children.*

F From *A Woman's Place*. Mrs Booth was born in 1900 and had four children. Here she is asked whether she wanted a large family:

Well, I mean, we never thought of it. They just came and that was it. I mean, I was as green as grass when I got married and I don't think me husband were much ... brighter. No, they just came.

53

G From *A Woman's Place*. Mrs Heron was born in 1889 and lived in Lancaster. Her mother had eleven children, all born before 1902. Here she is asked who helped her mother with the births:

> Oh, I think we managed. Martha used to come, the midwife … she wasn't certified or anything but she was one of the good old midwives and it was only a few shillings for a confinement. I've heard m'mother say that she used to give her sixpence a week until she got it paid off. She was a grand old lass.

certified = registered as a qualified and properly trained midwife. Until 1902 it was not compulsory to be registered, and anyone could be a midwife.
confinement = childbirth

H From *A Woman's Place*. This woman from Preston, was born in 1900 and had four children:

> Well, my first baby was born on a Tuesday and on the Saturday (before) I said to my husband, 'I am bothered.' and he said, 'What's the matter?' And I said, 'How can a baby come out?' You know, you had a brown mark there and I thought how can a baby come out there, how will it? I was terrified of this bursting, you know. He said, 'Well what do you mean?' … He said, 'But they don't come out there.' I said, 'Where do they come out?' and he said, 'Where it goes in.' And do you know, I nearly died. Well I was more het up than ever. How could it? … and I really think I suffered more through ignorance; you do!

I From *A Woman's Place*. Mrs Pearce was born in 1899 and had six children during the 1920s and 1930s: two of them died. In this source she describes her visit to the hospital doctor to have her last pregnancy confirmed:

> There must have been tears in my eyes because I was thinking about keeping them. I loved children but it was the thought of keeping them. You want them to be as nice as others as well as feeding them. He said, 'It's no good crying now, it's too late!' I felt like saying that it wasn't the woman's fault all the time. You are married and you have got to abide by these things, you know. He (her husband) once said that if anybody had seen this squad in here, they would think that we had a wonderful time, but they don't know what I would have gone through to try to avoid it, you know. We never would take anything in them days. God had sent them and they had to be there. I'm not a religious person, but that were my idea.

J Part of an anonymous letter from a woman in 1915, collected by the Women's Cooperative Guild, *Maternity*:

> My grandmother had over twenty children; only eight lived to about fourteen years, only two to a good old age. A cousin (a beautiful girl) had seven children in about seven years; the first five died in birth, the sixth lived, and the seventh died and the mother also. What a wasted life! Another had seven children; dreadful confinements, two or three miscarriages, an operation for trouble in connection with the same. Three children died and the mother also quite young. There are cases all around us much worse.

K 'The New Doctor', a cartoon from 1893.

THE NEW DOCTOR

'THE *HIDEA* OF A YOUNG MAN LIKE THAT A-TELLING O' *ME* 'OW POOR PEOPLES' CHILDREN HOUGHTER BE FED AND LOOKED AFTER! WHY, I'VE BURIED FOURTEEN O' MY *OWN!*'

L From *Out of the Doll's House*. Marjorie Jones remembers going to an Infant Welfare Centre in Hornsey just before World War I with her mother and baby brother:

> The prams were left outside in the yard of this run-down, yellow brick building ... My mother didn't like the idea of going. I know that she was very tense about it. In those days we weren't used to coming in contact with nurses and doctors like we are now.

M *Photograph of a Mother and Child Clinic in the 1920s.*

N From *Out of the Doll's House*. Nellie Finley was a young mother in Deptford in the 1920s:

> I used to go by my own instincts or I used to go to my mother-in-law. She was very good, very clever with children and I used to copy her, do what she told me. In one ear, out the other with health visitors, definitely.

O From *Out of the Doll's House*. Hilda Bates was a health visitor between the wars, and recalls the suspicion of many mothers towards local authority clinics:

> They couldn't see why the government should want to register or take any interest in their child. And they wouldn't bring their children to the clinic every month as they were supposed to do. Anyway, the clinic was awful. It was a filthy, dirty public house and, although it wasn't used, it was smelly still. No windows open.

P From *Out of the Doll's House*. Dorothy Campbell was a health visitor in Birmingham in the 1930s:

> A lot of them came and then a lot of them thought the Public Health Department were interfering in their lives ... The people we really wanted – the very ignorant – often wouldn't come (to childbirth clinics). We wanted to teach them hygiene because a lot of people fed their babies from the milkman's milk which was delivered in a jug from a can. There was no pasteurisation of milk. Women had to be taught to sterilise their bottles.

Q From *Out of the Doll's House*. Josephine Barnes was a young doctor at University College Hospital, London in the 1930s:

> One did see some pretty horrific poverty, particularly in areas like the Caledonian Road where you'd have six families, each living on one of six floors, one water tap half way and a privy in the garden. I remember going to a house one Sunday evening to deliver a lady of her seventh child and the other six were sitting round in the room next door eating chips. There were no bedclothes on the bed, because they'd been pawned and were going to be taken out of pawn on Monday when the pay came in.

R *Photograph of a slum family in Bethnal Green, London in 1923.*

S From *A Woman's Place*. Mrs Pearce (see Source **E**) had her first confinement in 1923 in the lodgings where she and her husband lived in Preston:

> *Question:* 'They gave you chloroform at home, did they?'
> *Answer:* 'Yes. Well, it were a breech. They did turn me. She (her mother-in-law) said that she had never seen anything like it in her life. The nurse and doctor had both their sleeves rolled right up here. They were sweating. I was in bed about a fortnight and she looked after me while I was in bed. Because we couldn't afford to pay anybody else. After that ... my husband ... said, 'You are going away. I'm not having you messed about like that.' So after that, with the other ones, I went away. My sister was frightened to death of hospitals. I thought, if she had gone through what I did at first, then she would want to go in hospital.'

breech = a baby born buttocks first rather than head first

55

T From *Out of the Doll's House*. Ada Finney worked on a gynaecological ward during the 1930s, and was well aware of the great risk of puerperal fever (childbirth fever):

> There were absolutely no antibiotics then, absolutely nothing and we used to take any septic cases from the maternity unit and we lost three mothers in a week.

U From *Out of the Doll's House*. Dorothy Campbell returned to work as a health visitor in Birmingham in 1956 after a 15 year break:

> I saw women from the problem families that I'd first seen when they were five years old; I saw them at twenty bringing their own babies spotlessly clean to the clinic, making sure the children had the right amount of teeth and they all had their injections and intelligence tests and hearing tests and so on. Of course, they'd been brought up to come to the ante-natal clinic, you see, so they had a better start than their grandmothers.

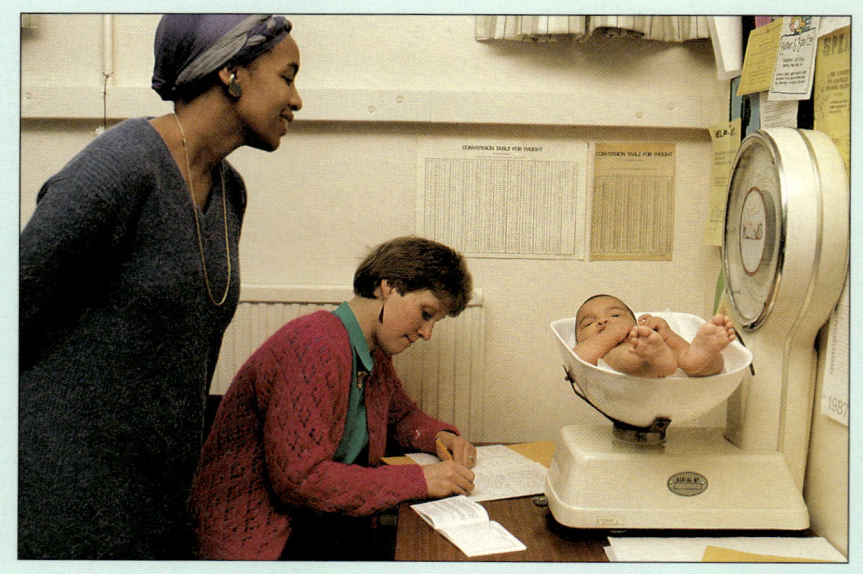

W *A modern baby clinic*

V From *The Position of Women*, by Richard Titmuss, 1956:

> ... the typical working-class mother of the 1890s, married in her teens or early twenties and experiencing ten pregnancies, spent about fifteen years in a state of pregnancy and in nursing a child for the first year of its life. She was tied, for this period of time, to the wheel of childbearing. Today, for the typical mother, the time so spent would be about four years. A reduction of such magnitude in only two generations in the time devoted to childbearing represents nothing less than a revolutionary enlargement of freedom for women brought about by the power to control their own fertility.

Questions

1. Read Sources **B** and **C** carefully. What, according to the two writers, are the values of oral history, and why, despite this, do you think that historians might have to be cautious in their use of this kind of evidence? 6
2. Read Sources **D**, **E**, **F**, **G**, **H**, **I**, **J**, and **V**. What do they reveal about family size and the factors that influenced it earlier this century? 4
3. Examine Sources **K**, **L**, **M**, **N**, **O**, **P**, and **U** carefully. What evidence do they contain about attitudes to health officials?
4. What do Sources **Q**, **R**, **S**, and **T** reveal about the advantages and drawbacks of going to hospital to give birth during the 1920s and 1930s? 4
5. Describe briefly in your own words the changes shown in graphs (**i**), (**ii**) and (**iii**) in Source **A**. Then say how useful the other sources in the chapter are in explaining these changes. 10

Chapter 13 Cigarette smoking

An exercise in the interpretation and evaluation of advertisements as historical evidence

Almost all the sources in this chapter were designed to influence the people who saw them. Some advertisements were meant to encourage people to smoke, others to put people off smoking. Study them carefully then answer the questions that follow.

A *'The Smoke Idol', cartoon from 1855. The caption reads: 'It is estimated that during the year 1854, the sum expended in the United Kingdom in cigars and tobacco, and afterwards "lost in smoke", exceeded £8,000,000 sterling. This enormous sum exceeds the gross amount levied for the Poor Rate of the entire nation, and is about ten times as much as all the Missionary and Bible Societies put together raised in the same period!'*

B *'The New Woman', illustration from* Pick-me-Up Magazine, *1900.*

C *Capstan cigarettes, 1930.*

D *Craven A cigarettes, 1931.*

F *Soldiers relaxing during WWII.*

E *A still from the film* Philadelphia Story, *with James Stewart and Katharine Hepburn.*

G *Tobacco company sponsorship of sport in the 1980s.*

H *Graph of cigarette consumption in UK 1890–1988*

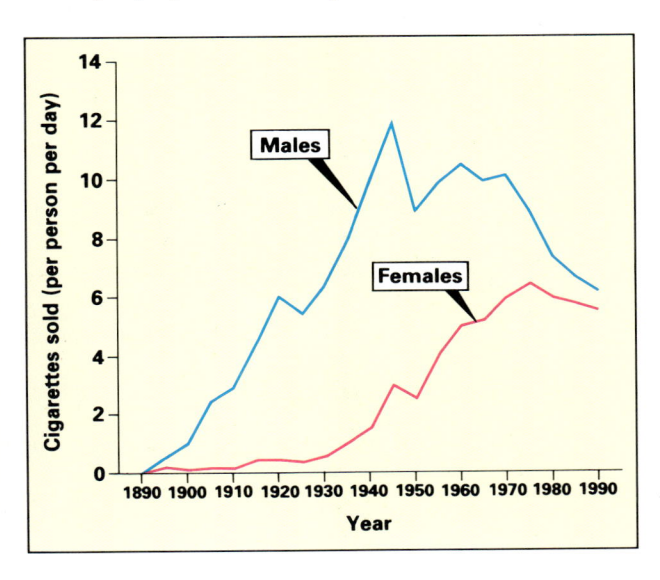

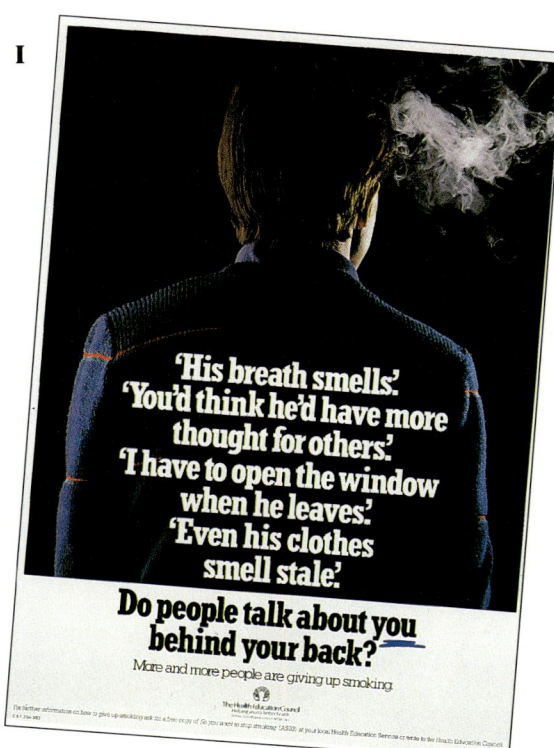

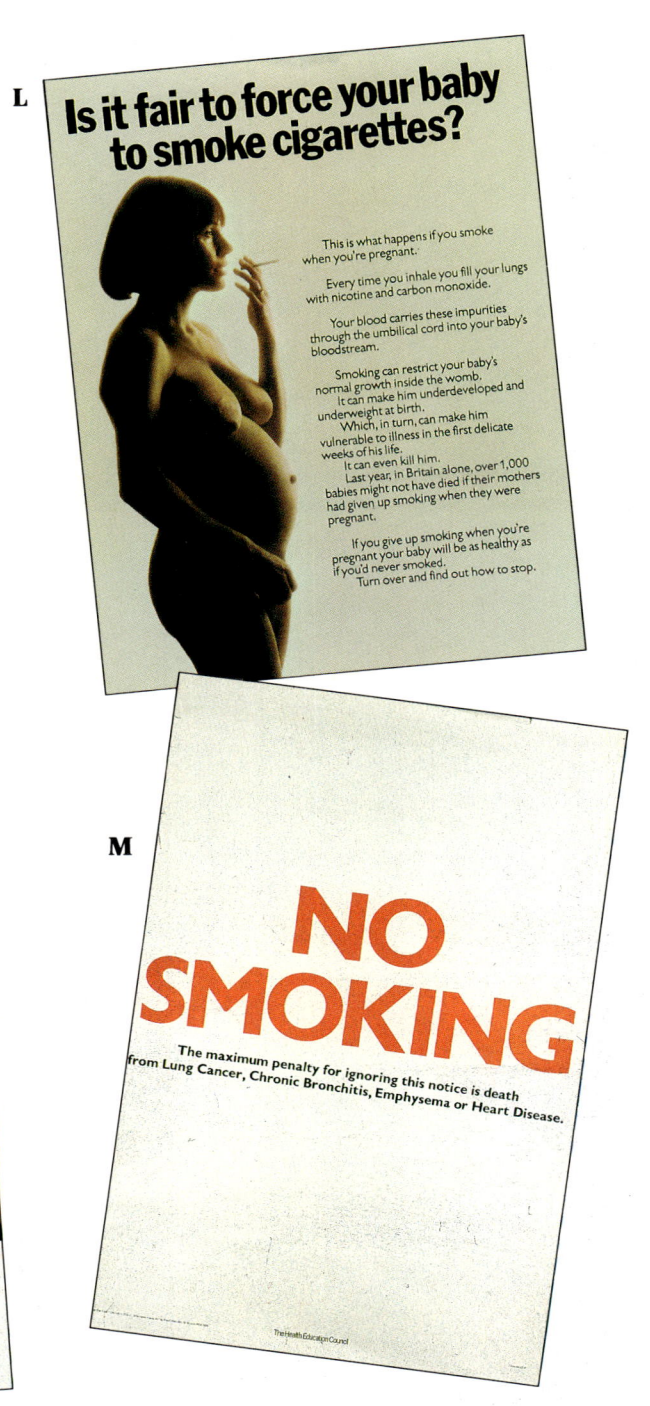

I 'His breath smells.' 'You'd think he'd have more thought for others.' 'I have to open the window when he leaves.' 'Even his clothes smell stale.' **Do people talk about you behind your back?** More and more people are giving up smoking.

J **No wonder smokers cough.** The tar and discharge that collects in the lungs of an average smoker.

K Please don't teach your children to smoke.

L **Is it fair to force your baby to smoke cigarettes?**

This is what happens if you smoke when you're pregnant.

Every time you inhale you fill your lungs with nicotine and carbon monoxide.

Your blood carries these impurities through the umbilical cord into your baby's bloodstream.

Smoking can restrict your baby's normal growth inside the womb. It can make him underdeveloped and underweight at birth.

Which, in turn, can make him vulnerable to illness in the first delicate weeks of his life.

It can even kill him.

Last year, in Britain alone, over 1,000 babies might not have died if their mothers had given up smoking when they were pregnant.

If you give up smoking when you're pregnant your baby will be as healthy as if you'd never smoked.

Turn over and find out how to stop.

M **NO SMOKING** The maximum penalty for ignoring this notice is death from Lung Cancer, Chronic Bronchitis, Emphysema or Heart Disease.

N

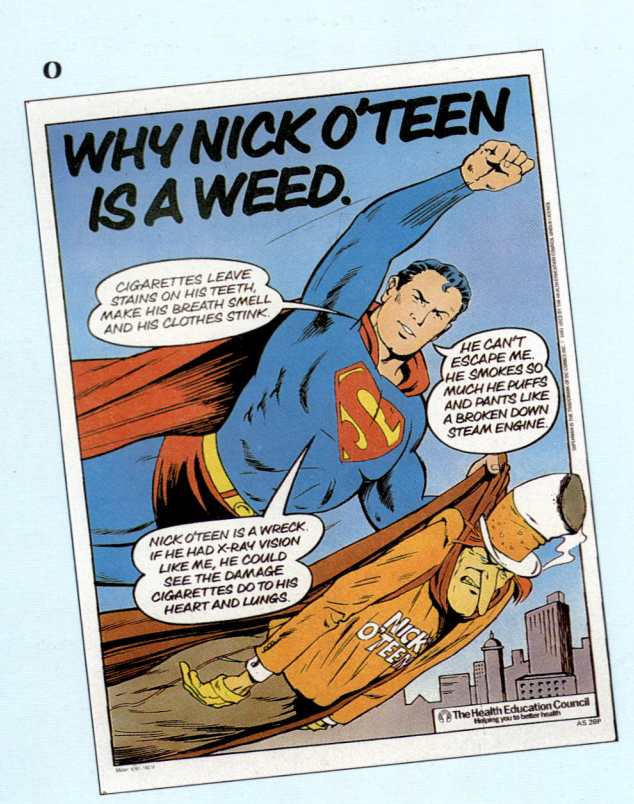

A lot of young men stop smoking suddenly.

O

WHY NICK O'TEEN IS A WEED.

P

Only one out of every three people smokes.
The other two choke.
Don't force your smoke down other people's throats.

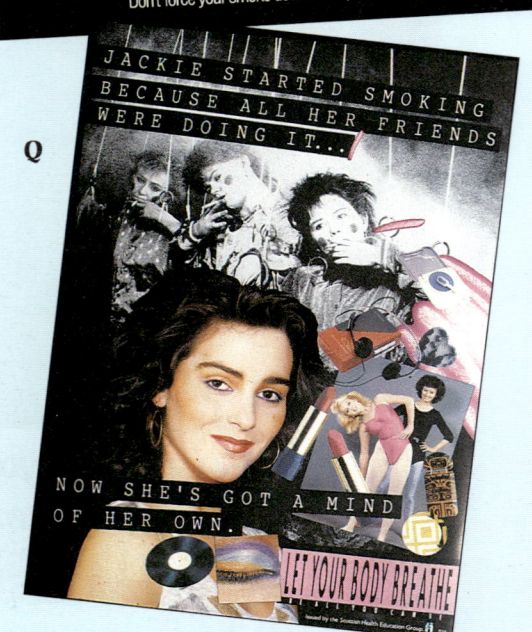

Q

JACKIE STARTED SMOKING BECAUSE ALL HER FRIENDS WERE DOING IT...
NOW SHE'S GOT A MIND OF HER OWN.
LET YOUR BODY BREATHE

R

PACESETTERS DON'T SMOKE

Questions

1. Study Sources **A**, **B**, **C**, **D**, **E**, **F**, **G**, and **H**. What evidence do they contain of changes in smoking and the factors that affected its popularity? Support your answer with references to each source. **8**
2. Sources **I**, **J**, **K**, **L**, **M**, **N**, **O**, **P**, **Q**, and **R** are all examples of anti-smoking advertisements. In each case, describe the way in which the designer of the poster was trying to influence those who saw it. **12**
3. Of what value are these advertisements in studying the history of smoking and health? Make reference to the advertisements to support your answer. **10**

60

Chapter 14 The role of medicine

An exercise in the interpretation of evidence

There have been some dramatic improvements in health over the last two centuries, and some equally dramatic advances in medical knowledge. But the extent to which these health improvements were the result of medical care has been a subject of controversy, which the sources in this chapter illustrate.

A From *The Development of Modern Medicine*, by Richard Shryock, 1948.

Bacteriological discoveries were especially calculated to arouse respect for the 'wonders of science'. There was something dramatic ... in the thought of doing battle against invading hosts. More than this, some of the first achievements of bacteriologists were of a decidedly spectacular character. The best illustration is afforded by the work of Pasteur, whose genius for legitimate publicity was almost as great as his scientific skill. In some cases his influence was due to the force of fear. Hydrophobia was a relatively rare but particularly terrifying disease. Pasteur apparently conquered it, and for a short time was the only one who could perform this miracle. The news flashed round the world, and frantic individuals from many nations rushed to Paris as to a saviour.

hydrophobia = another name for rabies, a highly dangerous disease that can be passed from animals to humans, for example by a dog bite

B In 1881 scientific medicine received an immense boost in prestige when the French scientist Louis Pasteur publicly demonstrated his newly developed vaccine to combat anthrax in sheep: he injected sheep with the anthrax bacilli, and those which he had not vaccinated quickly died. This account of the demonstration is from *The Microbe Hunters*, by Paul de Kruif, 1926:

The world received this news and waited, confusedly believing that Pasteur was a kind of Messiah who was going to lift from men the burden of all suffering. France went wild and called him her greatest son and conferred on him the Grand Cordon of the Legion of Honour. Agricultural societies, horse doctors, poor farmers ... all these sent telegrams begging him for thousands of doses of the life-giving vaccine.

C Photograph of objects from Pasteur's laboratory. (On the far right are some silkworm cocoons. In 1865 Pasteur used his microscope to find out what was killing silkworms and ruining the silk industry in France.)

D Painting of Pasteur in his laboratory in 1885, the year he developed his anti-rabies vaccine. The painting shows him examining a flask containing the spinal cord of a rabies-infected rabbit.

E In 1955 American scientists announced that a vaccine against the childhood infectious disease of polio had been proved effective. The public reaction is described in this extract from *Breakthrough: the Saga of Jonas Salk*, (the main scientist involved), by Richard Carter:

... more than a scientific achievement, the vaccine was a folk victory. People observed moments of silence, rang bells, honked horns, blew factory whistles, fired salutes ... drank toasts, hugged children, attended church, smiled at children, forgave enemies.

F From *The Social Transformation of American Medicine*, by Paul Starr, 1982:

The magic of science and money had worked. And if polio could be prevented, America had reasons to think that cancer and heart disease and mental illness could be stopped too. Who knew how long human life might be extended? Medical research might offer passage to immortality.

G From *The Development of Modern Medicine*, by Richard Shryock, 1948:

After about 1870 the mortality of one after another of the chief infectious diseases began to fall; and this process was accelerated in a remarkable manner during the first decades of the present century ... Smallpox, typhoid, tuberculosis, diphtheria, typhus, malaria, yellow fever and other plagues were checked or even eliminated in the half-century between 1870 and 1920. This was indeed the most impressive record in all medical history.

H Graphs showing the decline in infectious diseases in England and Wales and the dates of effective treatment becoming available.

(i) *Tuberculosis, 1850–1865*

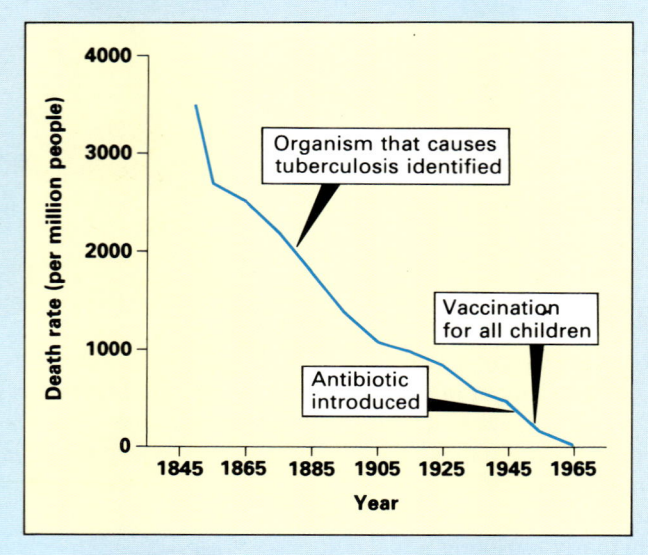

(ii) *Scarlet Fever, 1865–1965*

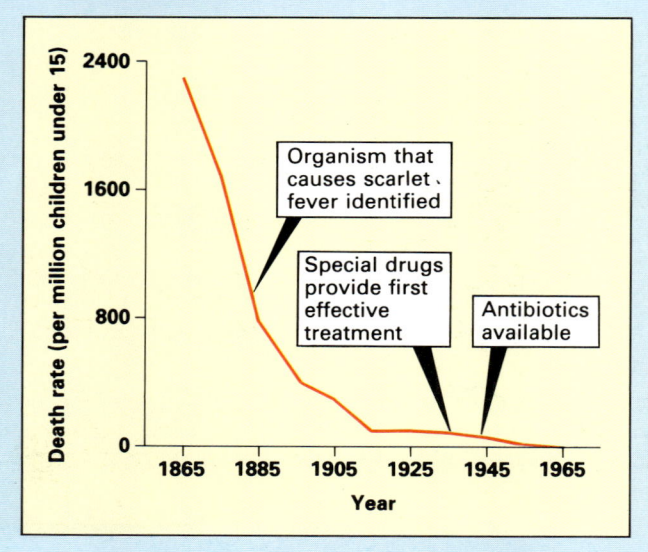

(iii) *Whooping Cough, 1855–1965*

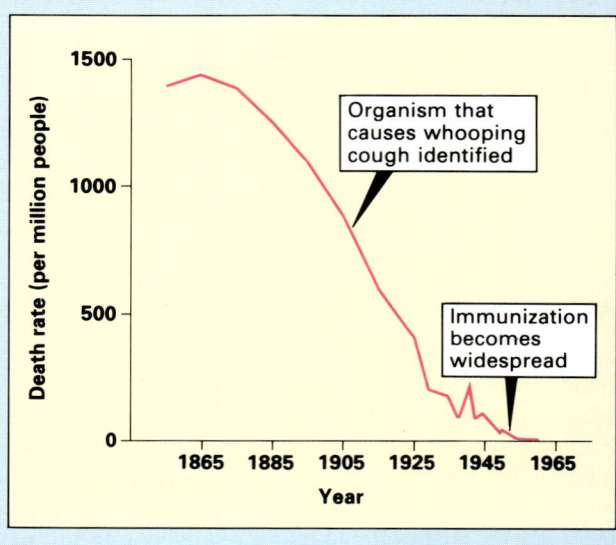

(iv) *Measles, 1855–1975*

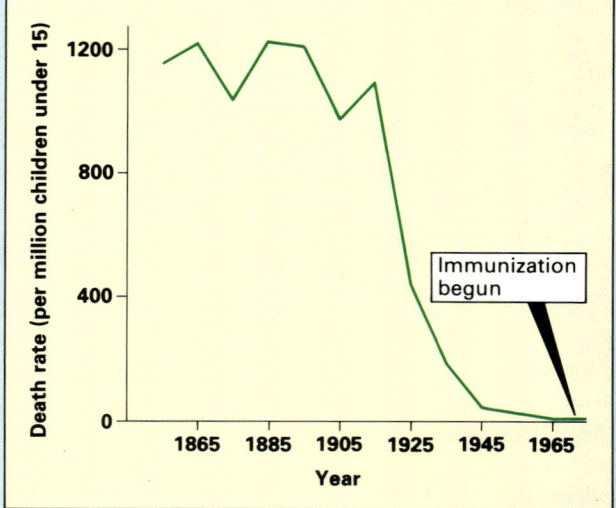

I From *An Introduction to Social Medicine*, by Thomas McKeown, 1966:

In descending order of importance the main influences responsible for the decline of mortality – our best index of improved health – since deaths were first registered in 1838 have been: (1) a rising standard of living, (2) hygienic measures, and (3) specific preventive and curative therapy.

J From *Mirage of Health*, by René Dubos, 1959:

... while modern science can boast of so many startling achievements in the health fields, its role has not been so unique and its effectiveness not so complete as is commonly claimed. In reality ... the monstrous specter of infection had become but an enfeebled shadow of its former self by the time serums, vaccines, and drugs became available to combat microbes ...

London slum-children queueing for free meals, about 1900

K *Modern photograph showing the food consumed in a year by an average British family*

L *Graph showing decline in air pollution, and decline in bronchitis, between 1963 and 1983 in Sheffield.*

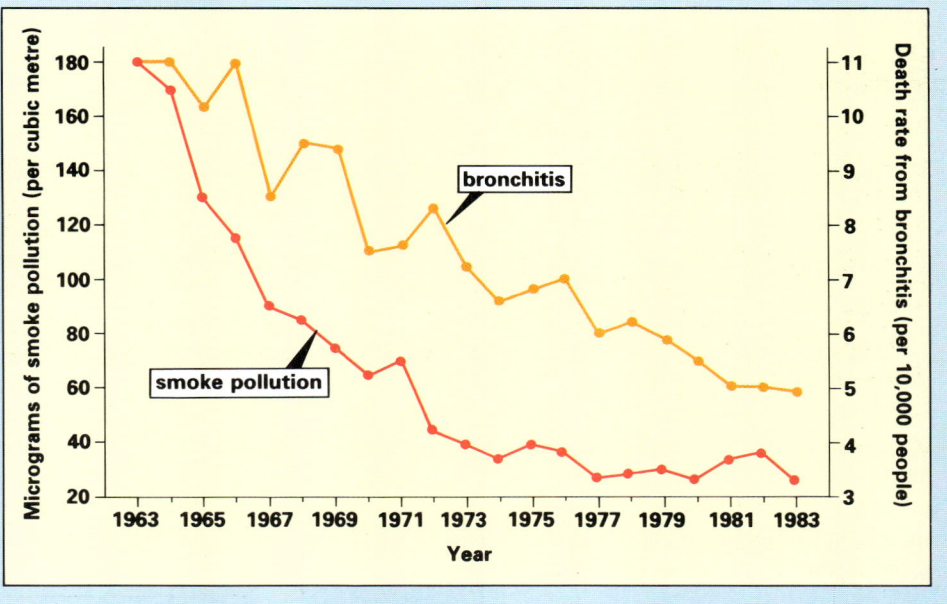

63

M *Photographs showing the effects of chimneys in Longton Staffordshire in 1910 (top) and in 1970 (bottom).*

P From *Mirage of Health*, by René Dubos, 1959:

Modern man ... now claims that the royal avenue to the control of disease is through scientific knowledge and medical technology ... He is encouraged to believe that money can create drugs for the cure of heart disease, cancer, and mental disease, but he makes no worth-while effort to recognize, let alone correct, the mismanagement of his everyday life that contribute to the high incidence of these conditions ... He laughs louder ... but one out of every four citizens will have to spend at least some months or years in a mental asylum. One may wonder indeed whether the pretense of superior health is not itself rapidly becoming a mental aberration. Is it not a delusion to proclaim the present state of health as the best in the history of the world, at a time when increasing numbers of persons in our society depend on drugs and on doctors for meeting the ordinary problems of everyday life?

O From *Limits to Medicine*, by Ivan Illich, 1976:

... medical intervention (is) one of the most rapidly spreading epidemics of our time. ... Every twenty-four to thirty-six hours, from 50 to 80 per cent of adults in the United States and the United Kingdom swallow a medically prescribed chemical. Some take the wrong drug; others get an old or contaminated batch, and others a counterfeit; others take several drugs in dangerous combinations. Some drugs are addictive, others mutilating ... In some patients, antibiotics induce a superinfection ... Unnecessary surgery is a standard procedure ... accidents seem to occur more often in hospital than in any other kind of place ... A military officer with a similar record of performance would be relieved of his command, and a restaurant or amusement centre would be closed by the police.

N From *The Decline of Mortality in Britain, 1870–1950*, by J. M. Winter, 1982:

When a doctor advises a change in diet or the removal of unsanitary debris, he may very well improve the survival chances of his patients. Simply because doctors do not require a medical education to make such statements is no reason to conclude that such indirect medical intervention was unimportant in the process of mortality decline.

Questions
1. Study Sources **A, B, C, D, E, F**, and **G**. What evidence do they contain concerning the prestige of scientific medicine from the late nineteenth century onwards?   10
2. Study Sources **H, I, J, K, L, M, N, O**, and **P**. From the evidence these sources contain, how far, in your opinion, have improvements in health and life expectancy been the result of improving medical treatment?   20